The Book of More Fun Facts

By the same author

Treasure Chest for Public Speaking
Treasure Chest of Virtue
Treasure Chest of Motivation
Treasure Chest of Classical Literature

Little Red Book Series

Little Red Book of Slang-Chat room Slang
Little Red Book of English Vocabulary Today
Little Red Book of Grammar Made Easy
Little Red Book of English Proverbs
Little Red Book of Prepositions
Little Red Book of Idioms and Phrases
Little Red Book of Euphemisms
Little Red Book of Effective Speaking Skills
Little Red Book of Writing Skills
Little Red Book of Verbal Phrases-1
Little Red Book of Verbal Phrases-2
Little Red Book of Synonyms
Little Red Book of Antonyms

A2Z Book Series

A2Z Quiz Book
A2Z Book of Origins

Others

The Book of Fun Facts
The Book of More Fun Facts
The Book of Firsts and Lasts
Read Write Right: Common errors in English

Fiction

Vilayti Pani: The Anglo-Indian Novel

The Book of More Fun Facts

Terry O'Brien

RUPA

Published by
Rupa Publications India Pvt. Ltd 2012
7/16, Ansari Road, Daryaganj
New Delhi 110002

Sales centres:
Allahabad Bengaluru Chennai
Hyderabad Jaipur Kathmandu
Kolkata Mumbai

ISBN: 978-81-291-1898-1

Second impression 2019

10 9 8 7 6 5 4 3 2

Typeset by Innovative Processors, New Delhi

Printed at Shree Maitrey Printech Pvt. Ltd, Noida

I dedicate this book to late Prof. A.P. O'Brien,
my father, friend, guide and mentor, who
inspired me to the canon of excellence:
re-imagining what's essential

Contents

1. Potpourri of Fun Facts 1
2. Statistics 16
3. People Factor 19
4. Animals 23
5. Religion 49
6. Entertainment Arena 50
7. Food and Drink 58
8. History 60
9. Literary World 64
10. Science 79
11. Sports 88
12. World of Business 92
13. Places 97
14. Odds and Ends 110
15. More Fun Facts 119
16. Household Trivia 121

Potpourri of Fun Facts

- **111,111,111 × 111,111,111 = 12,345,678,987,654,321**
- **160 cars can drive** side by side on the Monumental Axis in Brazil, the world's widest road.
- **315 entries in Webster's Dictionary** will be misspelled.
- **A cat has 32** muscles in each ear.
- **A giraffe can clean** its ears with its 21-inch tongue.
- **A giraffe can go without** water longer than a camel can.
- **A goldfish has a** memory span of three seconds.
- **A hedgehog's heart beats** 300 times a minute on average.
- **A Saudi Arabian woman** can get a divorce if her husband doesn't give her coffee.
- **A sneeze travels out your** mouth at over 100 m.p.h.
- **All of the clocks in the** movie "Pulp Fiction" are stuck on 4:20.
- **All porcupines** float in water.
- **Ancient Egyptians** slept on pillows made of stone.
- **An animal epidemic** is called an *epizootic*.
- **An average person laughs** about 15 times a day.
- **Babies are born without** knee caps. They don't appear until the child reaches 2-6 years of age.
- **Barbie's measurements if she** were life size: 39-23-33.
- **Bats always turn left** when exiting a cave.
- **Bubble gum** contains rubber.

- **Camel's milk** does not curdle.
- **Canada is an Indian** word meaning "Big Village".
- **Cat's urine glows** under a blacklight.
- **Cats can produce over** one hundred vocal sounds, while dogs can only produce about ten.
- **Columbia University** is the second largest landowner in New York City, after the Catholic Church.
- **Donald Duck** comics were banned from Finland because he doesn't wear pants.
- **Einstein couldn't speak fluently** when he was nine. His parents thought he might be retarded.
- **Every time Beethoven** sat down to write music, he poured ice water over his head.
- **February 1865 is the** only month in recorded history not to have a full moon.
- **Fingernails grow nearly 4 times** faster than toenails.
- **Giraffes** have no vocal cords.
- **Goethe couldn't stand the sound** of barking dogs and could only write if he had an apple rotting in the drawer of his desk.
- **If NASA sent birds into** space they would soon die; they need gravity to swallow.
- **In 1983, a Japanese artist** made a copy of the Mona Lisa completely out of toast.
- **In Kentucky, 50 per cent** of the people who get married for the first time are teenagers.
- **In Los Angeles,** there are fewer people than there are automobiles.
- **In the great fire of London** in 1666 half of London was burnt down but only 6 people were injured.
- **It takes a lobster approximately** seven years to grow to be one pound.
- **It takes about a half** a gallon of water to cook macaroni, and about a gallon to clean the pot.

- **It's impossible to sneeze** with your eyes open.
- **Kotex was first manufactured** as bandages, during WWI.
- **Leonardo Da Vinci** invented the scissors.
- **Lightning strikes about 6,000** times per minute on this planet.
- **Many hamsters only** blink one eye at a time.
- **Most cows give more milk** when they listen to music.
- **No word in the English language** rhymes with *month, orange, silver, and purple.*
- **Non-dairy** creamer is flammable.
- **One of the reasons marijuana** is illegal today is because cotton growers in the 1930's lobbied against hemp farmers—they saw it as competition. It is not as chemically addictive as is nicotine, alcohol, or caffeine.
- **Our eyes are always** the same size from birth, but our nose and ears never stop growing.
- **Owls are one** of the only birds who can see the color blue.
- **Peanuts are one** of the ingredients of dynamite.
- **Penguins can jump** as high as 6 feet in the air.
- **Playing cards were issued** to British pilots in WWII. If captured, they could be soaked in water and unfolded to reveal a map for escape.
- **Reindeer like** to eat bananas.
- **Research indicates that mosquitoes** are attracted to people who have recently eaten bananas.
- **Rubber bands** last longer when refrigerated.
- **Sherlock Holmes** never said "Elementary, my dear Watson."
- **Sigmund Freud** had a morbid fear of ferns.
- **"Stewardesses"** is the longest word that is typed with only the left hand.
- **The average person** falls asleep in seven minutes.

- **The average person** has over 1,460 dreams a year.
- **The average person** is about a quarter of an inch taller at night.
- **The average person's** left hand does 56 per cent of the typing.
- **The combination "ough"** can be pronounced in nine different ways. The following sentence contains them all: "A rough-coated, dough-faced, thoughtful ploughman strode through the streets of Scarborough; after falling into a slough, he coughed and hiccoughed."
- **The condom - made originally of linen -** was invented in the early 1500s.
- **The cruise liner,** Queen Elizabeth II, moves only six inches for each gallon of diesel that it burns.
- **The Earth weighs around** 6,588,000,000,000,000,000,000 tons.
- **The electric chair was** invented by a dentist.
- **The elephant is the** only mammal that can't jump.
- **The glue on Israeli** postage stamps is certified kosher.

- **The housefly hums** in the middle octave, key of F.
- **The longest one-syllable** word in the English language is "screeched."
- **The longest word** in the English language, according to the Oxford English Dictionary, is pneumonoultramicroscopicsilicovolcanoconiosis. The only other word with the same amount of letters is pneumonoultramicroscopicsilicovolcanoconioses, its plural.
- **The microwave was invented** after a researcher walked by a radar tube and a chocolate bar melted in his pocket.
- **The name for Oz** in the "Wizard of Oz" was thought up when the creator, Frank Baum, looked at his filing cabinet and saw A-N, and O-Z, hence "Oz."

- **The name Jeep came** from the abbreviation used in the army for the "General Purpose" vehicle, G.P.
- **The name Wendy** was made up for the book "Peter Pan."
- **The national anthem** of Greece has 158 verses. No one in Greece has memorised all 158 verses.
- **The only nation whose** name begins with an "A" but doesn't end in an "A" is Afghanistan.
- **The state of Florida** is bigger than England.
- **The word "Checkmate"** in chess comes from the Persian phrase "Shah Mat," which means "the king is dead".
- **The word "samba"** means "to rub navels together."
- **The world population of** chickens is about equal to the number of people.
- **The worlds oldest piece** of chewing gum is 9000 years old.
- **There are 336 dimples** on a regulation golf ball.
- **There are more chickens** than people in the world.
- **There are only four words** in the English language which end in "-dous": tremendous, horrendous, stupendous, and hazardous.
- **There are two credit cards** for every person in the United States.
- **Thomas Edison, lightbulb inventor,** was afraid of the dark.

- **Tigers have striped skin,** not just striped fur.
- **To escape the grip** of a crocodile's jaws, push your thumbs into its eyeballs—it will let you go instantly.
- **Two-thirds of the world's** eggplant is grown in New Jersey.
- **When snakes are born** with two heads, they fight each other for food.

- **Windmills always turn counter-clockwise.** Except for the windmills in Ireland.
- **Winston Churchill was born** in a ladies' room during a dance.
- **Women's hearts** beat faster than men's.
- **You blink over** 20,000,000 times a year.
- **You can only smell** 1/20th as well as a dog.
- **You're born with 300 bones,** but when you get to be an adult, you only have 206.
- **You're more likely** to get stung by a bee on a windy day than in any other weather.
- **Your heart beats over** 100,000 times a day.
- **Your ribs move about** 5 million times a year, everytime you breathe.
- **Your right lung takes** in more air than your left one does.
- **Barack Obama:** his wife Michelle is codenamed *Renaissance.*
- **In the UK, Barack Obama** has been codenamed with a Hindi word 'Chalaque' (smart Alec).
- **In 2002, the most** popular boat name in the U.S. was *Liberty.*
- **One out of 20 people** have an extra rib.
- **44 per cent of kids watch television** before they go to sleep.
- **In 1865, the U.S. Secret Service** was first established for the specific purpose to combat the counterfeiting of money.
- **Every three days a human** stomach gets a new lining.
- **Mars is the home** of Olympus Mons, the largest known volcano in our solar system.
- **The gastric flu** can cause projectile vomiting.
- **Cinderella is known** as *Rashin Coatie* in Scotland, *Zezolla* in Italy, and *Yeh-hsien* in China.

- **The Great Pyramids used** to be as white as snow because they were encased in a bright limestone that has worn off over the years.
- **A monkey was once tried** and convicted for smoking a cigarette in South Bend, Indiana.
- **There are six million** parts in the Boeing 747-400.
- **Baskin Robbins plain vanilla** ice cream is the number one selling flavour and accounts for a quarter of their sales.
- **Elizabeth Taylor has appeared** on the cover of *Life* magazine more than anyone else.
- **The typical lead pencil** can draw a line that is thirty five miles long.
- **The word "toy"** comes from an old English word that means "*tool*."
- **Smokers are twice as** likely to develop lower back pain than non-smokers
- **Humans are born** with 300 bones in their body, however when a person reaches adulthood they only have 206 bones. This occurs because many of them join together to make a single bone.
- **The reason why hair** turns grey as we age is because the pigment cells in the hair follicle start to die, which is responsible for producing "melanin" which gives the hair colour.
- **No piece of paper** can be folded in half more than 7 times.
- **A one ounce milk** chocolate bar has 6 mg of caffeine.
- **Colour is not an indicator** for the taste or ripeness in cranberries.
- **Each year there are** approximately 20 billion coconuts produced worldwide.
- **A chicken with red** earlobes will produce brown eggs, and a chicken with white earlobes will produce white eggs.
- **Not all polar bears hibernate;** only pregnant female polar bears do.

- **There is a restaurant** in Stockholm that only offers all-garlic products. They even have a garlic cheesecake.
- **The Koala bear** is not really a bear, but is really related to the kangaroo and the wombat.
- **The word "comet"** comes from the Greek word "*kometes*" meaning long hair and referring to the tail.
- **Colgate faced a big** obstacle marketing toothpaste in Spanish speaking countries. *Colgate* translates into the command "go hang yourself."
- **The cross bow was** invented by the Chinese and records of its usage goes back to as far as the Three Kingdom Period.
- **One-third pound stalk** of broccoli contains more vitamin C than 204 apples.
- **The Flintstones cartoon** was the first thirty-minute cartoon to be aired during prime time.
- **The abbreviation Xmas for** the word Christmas is of Greek origin. Since the word for Christ in the Greek language is *Xristos*, which starts with the letter "X," they started putting the X in place of Christ and came up with the short form for the word Christmas.
- **Dipsomania refers to an insatiable** craving for alcoholic beverages.
- **China has more English** speakers than the United States.
- **The Ancient Greek women** made a type of cheek blush by painting their cheeks with herbal pastes which was made out of crushed berries and seeds.
- **Japan has approximately 200** volcanoes and is home to 10 per cent of the active volcanoes in the world.
- **The only South East Asian** country that has never been colonised by a western power is Thailand.
- **In 1631, two London** Bible printers accidentally left the word "*not*" out of the seventh commandment, which then read, "*Thou shalt commit adultery.*" This legendary book is now known as the "*Wicked Bible.*"

- **Irish Wolfhound dogs have** a short lifespan and live about 7-8 years.
- **When Queen Elizabeth I** of England died she owned over 3,000 gowns.
- **Female alligators lay about** 40 eggs that hatch in 60 - 70 days.
- **The nickname for a Japanese** businessman is "Salaryman."
- **Emus cannot** walk backwards.
- **The external tank on space** shuttles is not painted. It is the only part of the shuttle that is lost after launch, so it is not necessary to worry about metal corrosion.
- **Infants spend more time** dreaming than adults do.
- **The famous Casanova** (Giacomo Casanova) was a librarian for many years before he died.
- **The only species of turtle** that lives in the open ocean is the sea turtle.
- **Toronto was the first city** in the world with a computerised traffic signal system.
- **Seniors who drink a cup of coffee** before a memory test score higher than those who drink a cup of decaffeinated coffee.
- **Venus is the only planet** that rotates clockwise.
- **Some octopuses** have been known to eat their arms off when they are exposed to stressful situations.
- **The skeleton of a spider** is located on the outside of the body. The name for this is *exoskelton.*
- **The letter J does not** appear anywhere on the periodic table of the elements.
- **The words "abstemious,"** and "facetious" both have all the five vowels in them in order.
- **French soldiers during World War I** had the nickname "*poilu*" which translates to "hairy one."
- **Former U.S. President William Taft** converted the White House stable into a four car garage in 1909.

- **Some snails** live on branches in trees.
- **The youngest** pope was 11 years old.
- **Did you know you** share your birthday with at least 9 other million people in the world.
- **The longest chapter in the Bible is Psalm 119,** which has 176 verses.
- **During the First World War,** cigarettes were handed out to soldiers along with their rations.
- **Walt Disney had originally** suggested using the name *Mortimer Mouse* instead of *Mickey Mouse.*
- **The smile is the most** frequently used facial expression. A smile can use anywhere from a pair of 5 to 53 facial muscles.
- **The right lung of a human** is larger than the left one. This is because of the space and placement of the heart.
- **The pound key (#)** on the keyboard is called an *octothorpe.*
- **The chemical name** for caffeine is 1,3,7-trimethylzantihine.
- **In Belgium,** there is a museum just for strawberries.
- **The Simpsons is the longest** running prime-time animated series on television history.
- **The more a person** struggles to get out of quicksand the faster they will sink. Staying still, and being calm will actually make the body float in the quicksand because the body is less dense than the quicksand is.
- **Pumpkins contain** potassium and vitamin A.
- **Pepsi got its name** from the ingredient pepsin, which is said to aid in digestion, however, it is not known.
- **Rabbits can live** up to ten years.
- **The average life span** of a single red blood cell is 120 days.
- **The last thing Elvis Presley** ate before he died was four scoops of ice cream and 6 chocolate chip cookies.

- **Some Chinese chopsticks contain** gold as on of their materials.
- **The watch was invented** by Peter Henlein of Nuremberg in 1510.
- **The concept of Boxing Day,** which is on December 26th, was to give boxes of food and clothing to the poor. It is now viewed in some countries as a time to get merchandise from stores at reduced prices.
- **Every year, Burger King** restaurants prepare over 950,000 pounds of bacon for their breakfast customers.
- **Isaac Newton** used to be a member of parliament.
- **Dumbest Dog:** Afghan hound.
- **At just four years** old Mozart was able to learn a piece of music in half an hour.
- **The word "diamond"** comes from the Greek word "*adamas*," which means "unconquerable."
- **The Basenji dog** is the only dog that is not able to bark.
- **There is a dog** museum in St. Louis, Missouri.
- **The palms of your** hands and the soles of your feet cannot tan, or grow hair.
- **A rabbit** is not able to vomit.
- **Niagara Falls actually stopped** flowing back in 1848 for about 20 hours because there was ice that was blocking the Niagara River.
- **The world's first underground** was the London Underground in 1863. It has 275 stations and 253 miles of track.
- **The first American president** to deliver a speech over the radio was Warren G. Harding.
- **The human body makes** anywhere from 1 to 3 pints of saliva every 24 hours.
- **Cheetahs are the fastest** land animal and can reach speeds up to 72mph.

- **The *purpose of tonsils*** is to destroy foreign substances that are swallowed or breathed in.
- **One of the most dangerous** insect in the world is the common housefly. They carry and transmit more diseases than any other animal in the world.
- **The only popcorn museum** in the world is lcoated in Marion, Ohio, USA.
- **Any animal that has skin** hair or fur can get dandruff, but in animals it is called "*dander*."
- **In 1893, the first** mosque in the United States was built.
- **Apples are part** of the rose family.
- **Enamel is hardest substance** in the human body.
- **A leech** has 32 brains.
- **Thomas Edison designed** a helicopter that would work with gunpowder. It ended up blowing up and also blew up his factory.
- **In the late 1800s,** washing machines and butter churners were sometimes powered by dogs walking on treadmills.
- **The sloth moves so** slowly that green algae grows in the grooves of their hair.
- **There are 50 per cent more** males that are left handed compared to females.
- **Carbon monoxide can kill** a person in less than 15 minutes.
- **The Nobel Peace prize** was first awarded in 1901 to Jean Henry Dunant, who was the founder of the Swiss Red Cross.
- **The wheelbarrow** was invented by the Chinese.
- **The colour blue** has a calming effect. It causes the brain to release calming hormones.
- **Crabs have very small** hairs on their claws and other parts of their body to help detect water currents and vibrations.
- **Duracell, the battery-maker,** built parts of its new international headquarters using materials from its own waste.

- **A common drink for Tibetans** is Butter Tea which is made out of butter, salt, and brick tea.
- **McDonald restaurants serve food** and drink to an amazing 43 million customers on a daily basis.
- **The game Monopoly was once** very popular in Cuba; however, Fidel Castro ordered that all games be destroyed.
- **During the era of Louis XIV,** women used lemons to redden their lips.
- **70 per cent of the poor people** in the world are female.
- **The adult human body** requires about 88 pounds of oxygen daily.
- **The word Nike comes** from Greek Mythology. *Nike* is the goddess of victory and was often depicted as a small winged figure whom the goddess Athene carried.
- **Leaving the water running** while brushing your teeth can waste four gallons of water in a minute.
- **The word Spain means** "*the land of rabbits.*"
- **In 1936, the first practical** helicopter was invented. It was the German Focke-Wulf Fw 61.
- **The fat that comes from sheep,** which is called *tallow,* can also be used to produce soap and candles.
- **In Britain, one out** of every four potatoes is eaten in the form of french fries.
- **In the movie Psycho** by Alfred Hitchcock, chocolate syrup was used for blood in the shower scene.
- **When the only queen** ant dies, so does the entire colony, because no new workers are born.
- **The Dutch people** are known to be the tallest people in Europe.
- **It has been suggested** that shepherds are responsible for inventing the game golf. It is said that they used to use their staffs to hit the stones.
- **There are about 6,800** languages in the world.

- **Studies have shown that** by putting on slow background music it can make a person eat food at a slower rate.
- **By walking an extra 20 minutes every day,** an average person will burn off seven pounds of body fat in an year.
- **The name of the first menthol** cigarette in the United States was "*Spud.*"
- **In a lifetime,** an average human produces 10,000 gallons of saliva.
- **Braces were first invented** by Pierre Fauchard in 1728. The braces were made by a flat strip of metal, which was connected to the teeth by thread.
- **Marilyn Monroe** had six toes.
- **The word "Nazi"** is actually an abbreviation for *Nationalsozialistische Deutsche Arbeiterpartei*, which refers to the National Socialist German Workers Party.
- **The unique characteristics** of Barbie dolls in Japan are that they have their lips closed with no teeth showing.
- **The Coca Cola company** offers more than 300 different beverages.
- **Neptune was the first planet** in our solar system to be discovered by mathematics.
- **Camel is considered** unclean meat in the Bible.
- **To be born on Sunday** was considered a sign of great sin during the Puritan times.
- **The citrus soda "7 UP"** was created in 1929. The original name of the popular drink was "*Bib-Label Lithiated Lemon-Lime Soda*", but it got changed to "7 UP."
- **Pluto is the only** planet in our solar system that has not been visited by a spacecraft.
- **The markings that are** found on dice are called "*pips.*"
- **Nerve cells can travel** as fast as 120 metres per second.
- **It is said that grapefruit** got its name because it grows like grapes in clusters. One cluster can have up to 25 grapefruits.

- **Women are four times** more likely to have foot problems than men.
- **In 1783, the hot** air balloon was invented in France.
- **The longest U.S.** highway is Route 20, which is over 3,365 miles.
- **The largest LEGO castle** that was ever built was built with 400,000 LEGO bricks and was 4.45 m x 5.22 m.
- **Every day 2,700 people** die of heart disease.
- **There are 10 million** bacteria at the place where you rest your hands at a desk.
- **The quills of a porcupine** are soft when they are born.
- **People have the tendency** to chew the food on the side that they most often use their hand.
- **In a lifetime,** an average driver will release approximately 912 pints of wind inside a car.
- **Women take three times** longer than men when using the toilet.
- **In 1886, Coca-cola** was first served at a pharmacy in Atlanta, Georgia for only five cents a glass. A pharmacist named John Pemberton created the formula for Coca-cola.
- **Whale oil was used** in some car transmissions until 1973.
- **Flamingos are able to fly** at a speed of approximately 55 kilometers an hour. In one night they can travel about 600 km.
- **Men are able** to read fine print better than women can.
- **Spiders usually** have eight eyes, but still they cannot see that well.
- **Women hearts** beat faster than men.
- **People generally** read 25 per cent slower from a computer screen compared to paper.
- **Jupiter is the fastest** rotating planet, which can complete one revolution in less than ten hours.
- **A chicken loses its** feathers when it becomes stressed.

- **Four per cent of the** US population are vegetarians.
- **Fifty-one per cent** of turns are right turns.
- **Fifty-five per cent** of motorbike accidents happen on the weekend.
- **Fifty-six per cent** of the video game market is adults.

- **Seven per cent** of Americans think Elvis is alive.
- **Seventy per cent** of all boats sold are used in fishing.
- **At 1.6 deaths** of every 1,000 persons, Qatar has the lowest death rate in the world.
- **It would take** more than 150 years to drive a car to the sun.
- **Men are 1.6 times** more likely to undergo by-pass surgery than women.
- **Meteorologists claim** they're right 85 per cent of the time.
- **Odds of being killed** by a tornado are one in two million.
- **Odds of being killed** by falling out of bed are one in two million.
- **Odds of being killed** in a car crash are one in 5,000.
- **Sweden has the** least number of murders annually.
- **The average person** speaks about 31,500 words per day.

- **The average person** will spend two weeks over their lifetime waiting for the traffic lights to change.
- **You are more likely** to get attacked by a cow than a shark.
- **Fifty-six per cent of the** video game market is adults.
- **811,000 faulty rolls of 35mm film** will be purchased this year.
- **Nine per cent of Americans have reported** having been in the presence of a ghost.
- **Ninety-five per cent of food poisoning** cases are never reported.
- **About one out of every 70 people** who pick their nose actually eat their bogies.
- **About five per cent of Americans claim** to have talked to the devil personally.
- **The average person spends about two years** on the phone in a lifetime.
- **The average person will spend two weeks** over their lifetime waiting for the traffic lights to change.
- **The murder rate in the** United States is 200 times greater than in Japan. In Japan no private citizen can buy a handgun legally.
- **A 'cakewalk' is actually an** American Negro dance.
- ***Thor* is the God of war in** Norse mythology; *Thursday* was named after him.
- ***Markka* is the currency** of Finland.
- **The order of animal called** *'chiroptera'* is better known as 'bats'.
- **The US Walter Hunt was** the inventor of the safety pin.
- ***The White Sea* is so called** as it is covered in ice for most of the year.

- ***Ovicide* is actually** sheep killing.
- **The expensive red spice that is** extracted from a crocus flower is *saffron.*
- **There are in total** seven deadly sins.
- **A US bomber plane** has been called B-52.
- **The snake hears** from its tongue.
- **Casanova was** a librarian.
- **Bones are kept** in an *ossuary*.
- **A horse is measured** in *'hands'*.
- **Ants and termites are the** favourite food of the *aardvark.*

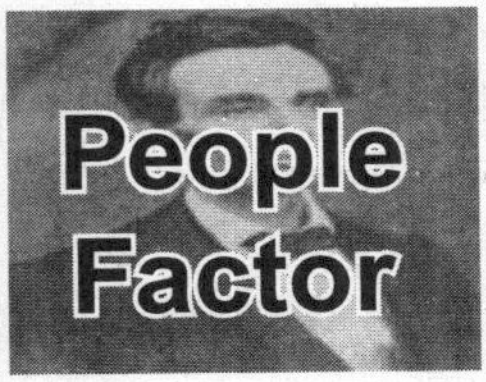

- **Robin Williams was** voted in high school the least likely to succeed.
- **Bill Cosby was** the first black man to win a best actor Emmy.

- **Keanu Reeves once** managed a pasta shop in Toronto.
- **Robert Kennedy was** killed in the Ambassador Hotel, the same hotel that housed Marilyn Monroe's first modeling agency.
- **Thomas Marshall** (1854-1925), US Vice President, once remarked, 'What this country needs is a good five-cent cigar.'
- **While at Harvard University**, Edward Kennedy was suspended for cheating in a Spanish exam.
- **Abraham Lincoln died** in the same bed that had been occupied by his assassin John Wilkes Booth.

- **Abraham Lincoln had** a nervous breakdown in 1836.
- **Abraham Lincoln has** a wart on his face.
- **All US presidents have** worn glasses; some of them just didn't like to be seen with them in public.
- **Andrew Johnson was** the only self–educated tailor. He is the only president to make his own clothes and those of his cabinet.

- **Former US President** Ronald Reagan once wore a Nazi uniform while acting in a film during his Hollywood days.
- **Four men were executed** for Abraham Lincoln's assassination.
- **Herbert Hoover was** the first US president to have a telephone in his office.
- **James Buchanan is** said to have had the neatest handwriting of all the presidents.

- **James Buchanan was** the only unmarried president of the US.
- **Louis XIV had 40** personal wigmakers and almost 1000 wigs.
- **President John Tyler** had 15 children.
- **President Teddy Roosevelt** died from an infected tooth.
- **Richard Nixon's favourite** drink was a dry martini.
- **Roosevelt was the** most superstitious president – he travelled continually but never left on a Friday. He also would not sit at the same table that held 13 other people.
- **Theodore Roosevelt finished** a speech he was delivering after being shot in the chest, before he accepted any medical help in 1812.

- **Thomas Jefferson anonymously** submitted design plans for the White House. They were rejected.
- **Thomas Jefferson, John Adams** and James Monroe all died on 4 July. Jefferson and Adams died at practically the same minute of the same day.
- **When the first Lady Eleanor Roosevelt** received an alarming number of threatening letters soon after her husband became President at the height of the Depression, the Secret Service insisted that she carry a pistol in her purse.
- **Queen Elizabeth I** was good friends with William Shakespeare.

- **According to Elvis's autopsy**, he had ten different drugs in his body at the time of his death.
- **Frank Sinatra was** once quoted as saying that rock 'n' roll was only played by 'cretinous goons'.
- No US president has been an only child.
- President Theodore Roosevelt was the first to announce to the world that Maxwell House coffee is 'Good to the last drop'.
- Prince Harry and Prince William are uncircumcised.
- **Andy Gracia was a** Siamese Twin.
- **Steven Seagal is** a 7th degree black belt in Aikido.
- **Tommy Lee Jonesand Vice President Al Gore** were freshman roommates at Harvard.

- **Although starring in many gangster** films, James Cagney started his career as a chorus boy.
- **John Forsythe was the voice** of the Angles' Charlie.
- **Micheal J Fox was born in** Edmonton, AB, Canada.

- **Sylvia Miles had the shortest performance** ever nominated for an Oscar with *Midnight Cowboy*. Her entire role lasted only six minutes.
- **Al Capone's famous ever (which earned him the nickname Scarface) was from an attack. The brother of a girl he had insulted attacked him with a knife, leaving him with three distinctive scars.**
- **Behram, an Indian thug, holds the record for most murders by a single individual. He strangled 931 people between 1790 and 1840 with a piece of yellow and white cloth called a *ruhmal*. The most by a woman is 610, by Countess Erzsebet Bathory of Hungary.**
- **Mass murderer Charles Manson recorded an album called Lie.**
- **While in Alcatraz, Al Capone was inmate #85.**

- **Abraham Lincoln's mother died when the family dairy cow ate poisonous mushrooms and Ms Lincoln drank the milk.**
- **David Rice Atkinson was President of the United States for exactly one day.**

- **Simon de Valera, who was born in the US, was** once president of Ireland.
- **Former US president Jimmy Carter had an operation for** haemorrhoids while he was in office.
- **President John Quincy Adams owned a pet alligator which** he kept in the East Room of the White House

- **Richard Nixon left instructions for 'California, Here I** come' to be the last piece of music played (slowly and softly) were he to die in office.
- **The only President to be head of a labour union** was Ronald Reagan.
- **US president Millard Fillmore's mother feared he** may have been mentally retared.
- **Princess Grace of Monaco was once on the** board of 20th Century-Fox.
- **Queen Berengaria (1191 A D) of England never lived in** or visited England.
- **Queen Victoria eased the discomfort of her** menstrual cramps by having her doctor supply her with marijuana.
- **Elvis Presley had a twin brother named** Garon, who died at birth, which is why Elvis's middle name was spelled Aron, in honour of his brother.
- **Elvis Presley received his US army discharge** on 5 March, 1960.
- **Elvis Presley was once appointed Special Agent of** the Bureau of Narcotics and Dangerous Drug.

- **Mick Jagger attended the London School of** Economics for two years.
- **Paul McCartney's mother was** a midwife.

Animals

- **Deer cannot** eat hay.
- **A donkey will sink** in quicksand but a mule won't.
- **A female ferret will** die if it goes on heat and cannot find a mate.
- **A group of hares** is called a husk.
- **A jackrabbit can** jump as high as 15 feet.

- **A mole can dig** over 250 feet of tunnel in a single night.
- **A single sheep's fleece** might well contain as many as 26 million fibres.
- **A species of earthworm** in Australia grows up to 10 feet in length.
- **An iguana can stay** under water for 28 minutes.
- **Basilisks are frequently** called Jesus Christ Lizards because of their ability to run on water.
- **Between 1902 and 1907** the same tiger killed 436 people in India.
- **Herons have been observed** to drop insects on the water and then catch the fish that surface for the bugs.
- **Jaguars are scared** of dogs.
- **Many hamsters only** blink one eye at a time.
- **No pearls of value** are ever found in North American oysters.
- **Rhinos are in the** same family as horses, and are thought to have inspired the myth of the unicorn.

- **Sea otters** have two coats of fur.
- **Slugs have** four noses.
- **Some ribbon worms** will eat themselves if they cannot find food.
- **The candlefish is** so oily that it was once burned for fuel.
- **The cells which** make up the antlers of a moose are the fastest growing animal cells in nature.
- **The electric eel** has an average discharge of 400 volts.
- **The female ferret** is referred to as a jill.
- **The giant cricket** of Africa enjoys eating human hair.
- **The guinea pig** originated in South America.
- **The leg bones of** a bat are so thin that no bat can walk.
- **The only continent** without reptiles or snakes is Antarctica.
- **The poison arrow frog** has enough poison to kill about 2,200 people.
- **The tuatara lizard** of New Zealand has three eyes – two in the centre of its head and one on top.
- **There are an average** of 50,000 spiders per acre in green areas.
- **When cornered, the** horned toad shoots blood from its eyes.
- **You can cut up** a starfish into pieces and each piece will grow into a completely new starfish.
- **Armadillos are the** only animal besides humans that can get leprosy.
- **Armadillos have four** babies at a time, and they are always the same sex.
- **It may take longer** than two days for a chick to break out of its shell.
- **Dinosaurs were among** the most sophisticated animals that ever lived on earth. They survived for nearly 150 million

years – 75 times longer than humans have now lived on earth.

- **It takes 11 truckloads** of wood to make a proper funeral pyre for a full-size elephant.
- **A 'winkle' is** an edible sea snail.
- **A baby baleen whale** depends on a mother's milk diet for at least six months.
- **It takes an average** of 345 squirts to yield a gallon of milk from a cow's udder.
- **It takes the deep-sea** clam 100 years to grow to a length of one-third inch.
- **Dolphins have killed sharks** by ramming them with their snouts.
- **Jackrabbits are powerful** jumpers. A 20 inch adult can leap 20 feet in a single bound.
- **Rattlesnakes gather in** groups to sleep through the winter. Sometimes up to 1,000 of them will coil up together to keep warm.
- **Kangaroo rats never drink** water. Like their relatives the pocket mice, they carry their own water source within them, producing fluids from the food they eat and the air they breathe.
- **Each day, 100 or more** whales are killed by fishermen.
- **Reptiles are never** slimy. Their scales have few glands, and are usually silky to the touch.
- **Kittens can clock an** amazing 31 miles per hour at full speed, and can cover about three times their body length per leap.
- **Koalas are marsupials**, not bears. They also have no tail or eyelids.
- **Elephants and short-tailed** shrews get by on only two hours of sleep a day.
- **Like the swiftest** of all antelopes, the impala can easily leap as far as 35 feet.

- **Sea sponges are** used in drugs for treating asthma and cancer.
- **Seals can withstand** water pressure of up to 850 pounds per square inch.
- Male **boars form** harems.

- **Male cockatoos can** be taught to speak, but females can only chirp and sing.
- **Male sea lions** may have more than 100 wives and sometimes go three months without eating.
- **Male western fence** lizards do push-ups on tree limbs as a courtship display for females.
- **The dodo, extinct less** than 100 years after being discovered by the Dutch in 1598, was not a prolific species. The female laid just one egg a year.
- **The domestic cat** is the only species able to hold its tail vertically while walking. Wild cats hold their tail horizontally, or tucked between their legs while walking.

- **The duckbill platypus** of Australia can store up to 600 worms in its large cheek pouches.
- **Skunks have more** than smell to protect themselves. They can withstand five times the snake venom that would kill a rabbit.
- **The elephant seal** is the heaviest seal in the world; males can reach 21 feet (six metres) in length and 8,800 pounds.
- **The elephant's closest** relative is the hyrax, which is found in the Middle East and Africa and is only about one foot long. Like its gigantic cousin, the hyrax has hoofed toes and a two – chambered stomach for digesting a vegetable diet.
- **We speak of a bale** of turtles, a clowder of cats, a charm of goldfinches, a gam of whales, a knot of toads and a streak of tigers.
- **Some sharks swim** in a figure eight when frightened.
- **Minnows have teeth** in their throats.

- **Some mantis shrimp** travel by doing backward somersaults.
- **The European eagle owl** is the largest owl in the world. It can measure 28 inches (70 centemetres) tall which a wingspan of five (150 centimetres) wide.
- **The eyes of some birds** weigh more than their brain. Likewise, their bones weigh less than their feathers.

- **South America's harpy** eagles eat monkeys. The birds build twig platforms in the treetops where they lay their eggs.
- **The killer whale**, or orca, is the fastest sea mammal. It can reach speeds up to 34 miles per hour (56 kilometers per hour) in pursuit of prey.
- **Corals are closely** related to jellyfish.
- **The Kodiak grizzly** bear is the world's largest meat-eating animal living on land. The Kodiak can weigh up to 500 pounds more than any other kind of bear.
- **The 20 million Mexican** free-tail bats from Bracken Cave, Texas, eat approximately 200 tons of insects nightly.
- **The largest bird egg** in the world today is that of the ostrich. Ostrich eggs are from six to eight inches long. Because of their size and the thickness of their shells, they take 40 minutes to hard-boil.
- **The first dinosaur** appeared around 225 or 230 million years ago. It was called the Staurikosaurus and it survived for about five million years.
- **The aardvark has** such a well- developed sense of hearing; it can detect and locate distant ants on a nighttime march.
- **The first dinosaur** to be given a name was the Iguanodon, found in Sussex, United Kingdom, in 1823. It was not the first dinosaur to be found.
- **The leech will gorge** itself up to five times its body weight and then just fall off its victim.
- **The flounder swims** sideways.

- **The loudest bird** in the world is the male bellbird, found in Central and South America. To attract mates, the male makes a clanging sound like a bell that can be heard from miles away.
- **The armour of the** armadillo is not as tough as it appears. It is very pliable, much like a human fingernail.

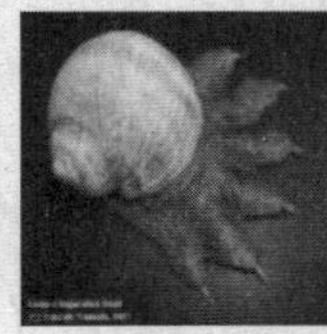

- **The giant African snail** grows to a foot long and reaches weights greater than a pound.
- **The giant flying foxes** that live in Indonesia have wingspans of nearly six feet.
- **There are eleven species** of hedgehog native of its life underground.
- **The male seahorse**, not the female, carries the embryo of the species. The female fills the male's brooch pouch with eggs, which remain in the swollen sac for a gestation period of eight to ten days.
- **There are lavender**, grey and blond skunks.
- **There are mice** that nest in trees. These creatures may spend their whole life without ever touching the ground.
- **The most venomous** of all snakes, the Inland Taipan, has enough venom in one bite to kill more than 200,000 mice.
- **The grey whale is** not really grey. It is black and just appears grey from a distance.
- **There are more than** 450 species of finches throughout the world.
- **There are no penguins** at the North Pole. In fact, there are no penguins anywhere in the Northern Hemisphere (outside of zoos). All 17 varieties of the bird are found below the equator, primarily in Antarctica.
- **There are no wild deer** of any kind in Australia, and the small red deer is the only one found in Africa.
- **The heaviest flighted** birds in the world are the great bustard at 40 pounds, the trumpeter swan at 37 pounds, the mute swan at 36 pounds, the albatross at 34 pounds and the whooper swan at 34 pounds.

- **There is just one** known species of ostrich in the world – it is in the order of Struthioniformes.
- **There once were more** sea lions on earth than people.
- **Thinking that a giraffe's** parents were a camel and a leopard, the Europeans once called the animal a 'camelopard'.
- **Thirty thousand monkeys** were used in the massive three-year effort to classify the various types of polio.
- **The woolly bats**, in West Africa, live in the large webs of colonial spiders.
- **Unlike most other** large cats, snow leopards cannot roar.
- **Walking catfish of** Florida can stay out of water for 80 days.

Interesting Facts About Butterflies

- **Butterflies can only fly** if their body temperature is above 86 degrees (30 degrees Celsius). This is why they sun themselves to warm up in cool weather.
- **As butterflies age,** the colour of the wings fades and their wings become ragged.
- **The top speed varies** among butterfly species (the poisonous varieties are slower than non-poisonous varieties). The fastest butterflies (some skippers) can fly at about 30 mph (50 km/h) or faster. Slow flying butterflies fly about 5 mph (8 km/h).
- **Butterflies undergo metamorphosis** where they change from a caterpillar into a butterfly.
- **Most species of butterfly** can see ultraviolet light.
- **The Monarch butterfly will fly** great distances when migrating.
- **Some butterflies are territorial** and will chase other butterflies out of their area.
- **There are between 15,000 and 20,000** species of butterflies worldwide.

- **Most butterflies live** in tropical regions, but they are found in every habitat on earth.

And More

- **A scallop has a total of** 35 eyes which are all blue.
- **A woodchuck breathes 2,100 times an hour, but** it only breathes 10 times an hour while it is hibernating.
- **Apart from humans, certain species of chimpanzee are the only animals** to experiment sexually. They have been known to 'wife swap' and indulge in group sex.

- **Belize is the only country** in the world with **a jaguar reserve.**
- **Certain fireflies emit a light so penetrating that it can** pass through flesh and wood

- **Estuarine crocodiles are the** biggest of all 26 species of the crocodilian family.
- **Frog-eating bats identify edible from poisonous frogs** by listening to the mating calls of male frogs. Frogs counter by hiding and using short, difficult to locate calls.

- **Giant flying foxes that live in Indonesia have wingspans** of nearly six feet.
- **Golden toads are so rare that a biological reserve has been** specifically created for them.
- **Hippopotami cannot** swim.
- **In Miami, Florida, roosting vultures have taken to snatching** poodles from rooftop patios.
- **In Michigan, USA, it is illegal to chain** an alligator to a fire hydrant.

- **Jackrabbits can reach a speed of 50 miles per hour and can leap** as high as five feet.
- **Male bees will try to attract sex partners** with orchid fragrance.

- **Mexican free-tailed bats sometimes fly up to two miles high to feed or to** catch tail-winds that carry them over long distance at speeds of more than 60 miles per hour.
- **Mongooses were brought to Hawaii to kill rats. This plan failed** because rats are nocturnal while the mongooses hunts during the day.
- **One species of antelope, the Sitatunga, c**an sleep under water.

- **Only 30 per cent of the famous Maryland blue crab** are actually from Maryland, the rest are from North Carolina and Virginia.
- **Parthenogenesis is the term used to describe the process by which certain** animals are able to reproduce themselves in successive female generations without intervention of a male of the species. At least one species of lizard is known to do so.
- **Tarantulas cannot** spin webs.

- **Tarantulas do not use muscles to move their legs.** They control the amount of blood pumped into them to extend and retract their legs.
- **The average cost of rehabilitating a seal after the Exxon Valdez oil** spill in Alaska was $80,000.

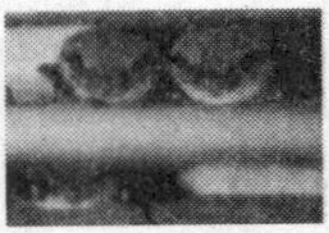

- **The brown myotis bat young when born** are equivalent to a woman giving birth to a 30lb baby.
- **The adult electric eel has enough electrical** power in it to power a house of about 1,200 square feet.

- **The honey badger can withstand hundreds of** African bee stings that would kill any other animals.
- **The Kansas city railroad used to stop their trains, in** 1868, to allow the passengers to shoot at passing buffalos.
- **The male gypsy moth can smell the virgin female gypsy** moth from eight miles away.

- **The Nile and Indo-Pacific saltwater crocodile are the only** two crocodiles that are considered true man-eaters.

- **The only female animal that has been antlers** is the **caribou.**
- **The only purple animal is the South** African Blesbok.
- **The poisonous copperhead smells like** fresh cut cucumbers.
- **The Portuguese Man-of-War 'jellyfish' tentacles have been** known to grow a mile in length, catching anything in its path by stinging its prey.

- **The tutara's metabolism is so slow they only** have to breathe once an hour.
- **The Weddell seal can travel under water for seven miles** without surfacing for air.

- **The world's smallest mammal is the bumblebee bat** of Thailand, weighing less than a penny.
- **There is no record of a non-rabid wolf** attack on a human.
- **To keep from being separated while sleeping, sea otters** tie themselves together with kelp, often drifting miles not so but to sea during the night.
- **When young, black sea basses are mostly female,** but at the age of five many switch sex and become male.
- **An armadillo can walk** under water.

- **It can take a deep-sea clam up to 100 years to reach 0.3 inches** (8 millimetres) in length. The clam is among the slowest growing, yet longest living species on the planet.
- **Despite its reputation for being finicky,** the average cat consumes about 127,750 calories a year, nearly 28 times its own weight in food and the same amount again in liquids.
- **It is estimated that a single toad** may catch and eat as many as 10,000 insects in the course of a summer.

- **It is estimated that manatees live** a maximum of 50 to 60 years.
- **It seems to biologists that, unlike their humpback whale relatives** whose under water song evolves from year to year, killer whales retain individual dialects unchanged over long periods, possibly even for life.

- **Disc-winged bats of Latin America** have adhesive discs on both wings and feet that enable them to live in unfurling banana leaves (or even walk up a window panel).

- **A baby caribouis is so swift it can easily outrun its mother** when it is only three days old.
- **Dogs that do not tolerate children are the St Bernard,** the Old English sheep dog, the Alsatian malamute, the bull terrier and the toy poodle.
- **It takes approximately 69,000 venom extraction from the coral snake** to fill a one-pint container.
- **It has been noted that the gender of a sea turtle is** determined by the temperature of the sand during incubation. Warm temperatures (greater than 29 degree C) produce more females; cooler temperatures (less than 29 degree C) produce more males.
- **Domesticated turkeys cannot fly. Wild turkeys** can fly for short distances at up to 55 miles per hour. Wild turkeys are also fast on the ground, running at speeds of up to 30 miles per hour.

- **Javelina herds require a territory** of at least one square mile.
- **Due to a retinal adaptation that reflect light back in the retina,** the night vision of tigers is six times better than that of humans.

- **During the 1800s, swan skins were used to make European ladies'** powder puffs and swan feathers were used to adorn fashionable hats.
- **Reaching sexual maturity in the wild at around 15 to 20 years of age, sturgeon** can live as long as 100 years. Mature females will produce millions of eggs every two to three years.

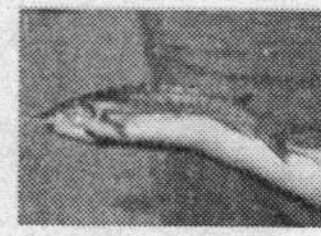

- **Reindeer have scent glands between their hind legs, The glands** help them leave scent trails for the herd.
- **Duroc is one American breed of hardy hog** having drooping ears- it was allegedly named after the horse owned by the hog's breeder.

- **During the mating season, male porcupines bristle their quills at each other chatter** their teeth in rage before attacking. All porcupines at this time become very vocal: grunting, whining, chattering, even barking and mewing at each other.
- **Earlier penguins were** capable of flight.

- **Lemon sharks grow a new set of teeth every two weeks.** They grow more than 24,000 new teeth every year.
- **Electric eels are not really eels but a kind of fish. Although they look like eels,** their internal organs are arranged differently.
- **Schools of South American (Pacific) Humbolt squid,** which reach 12 feet in length, have been known to strip 500ib marlins to the bone.

- **Scientists say that pigs unlike all domesticated** animals, arrive at solutions by thinking them through. Pigs can be- and have been- taught to accomplish almost any feat a dog can master, and usually in a shorter period of time.

- **Sea otters have the world's densest** fur- a million hairs per square inch.

- **Llamas are reported to be inquisitive, friendly animals. A llama greeting is** marked by softly blowing on each other. **According to animal experts, a soft blow to a person is** the Llama's way of saying hello.

- **Lungless salamanders are the largest group of** salamanders. They have no lungs or gills and breathe through their skin, which must be kept damp to allow oxygen in. If they dry out, they will die of suffocation.

- **Sharks' fossil records date back more than twice as long** as that of dinosaurs.
- **Sharks have sixth sense which enables them to detect** bioelectrical fields radiated by other sea creatures and to navigate by sensing changes in the earth's magnetic field.
- **Many seabirds that swallow fishes too large** for immediate digestion go about with the oesophagus filled. Apparently without discomfort, the tail of the fish sticks out of the bird's mouth.

- **The Egyptian vulture. This bird is one of the very few animals that, like man** manipulates objects as tools.
- **The electric eel is the most shocking animal on earth- no** animal packs such a big charge. If attacking a large prey, a nine-foot-long eel can discharge about 800 volts. One zap could stun a human. The larger the eel the bigger the charge.
- **The electric eel has thousands of electric cells running up** and down its tail. Vital use their electric sense to 'see'. Their electric sensors act like radar. They send out weak impulses which bounce off objects. Marine iguanas, saltwater crocodiles, sea snakes and sea turtles are the only surviving seawater-adapted reptiles.

- **So that it can pull its lithe body into a tight,** prickly little ball for defence, the **hedgehog** has a large muscle running along its stomach.

- **The electric organs in an electric eel** make up four-fifths of its body.
- **The emperor penguin is the largest type of penguin. It is also the deepest** diver, reaching depths of 870 feet (260 metres) and staying there for up to 18 minutes.
- **The emu is Australia's largest bird at a height of seven feet tall. It** can't fly, but it can swim and has the ability to run up to 40 miles per hour.

- **Migrating geese fly in a V-formation** to conserve energy. A goose's wings churn the air and leave an air current behind. In the flying wedge , each bird is in a position to get a lift from the current left by the bird ahead. It is easier going for all, except the leader. During a migration, gees are apt to take turns in the lead position.

- **Milk snakes lay about 13 eggs – in piles** of animal manure.

- **The enormous livers of basking sharks, which can account** for up to one-third of their body weight, produce a valuable oil used to lubricate engines and manufacture cosmetics.
- **Some species of freshwater eels migrate to the Sargosso Sea** in the Atlantic Ocean to mate. After laying up to 20 million eggs, the female eel dies. The baby eels hatched from the eggs then make their way back to fresh water.
- **More species of fish live in a single tributary of the Amazon River** than in all the rivers in North America combined.
- **More than million southern fur seals- 95 per cent** of the world's population- crowd onto the shores of South Georgia Island each summer. Half the world's population of southern elephant seals also come to the island to mate.

- **The Everglades kite bird, in Florida,** will only eat apple snails. The kites are becoming rare because as the Everglades dry up, the apple snails are dying out.

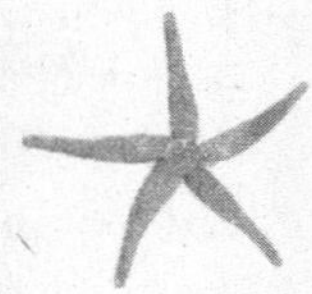

- **Some species of rain forest birds migrate every summer** from South America to Canada to breed.
- **Some species of starfishhave** as many as 50 appendages.

- **Starbuck, a Canadian bull who sired 200,000 dairy cows** and an equal number of bulls in his life, earned an estimated $25 million before he died in 1998. After his death, his frozen semen was still selling for $250 a dose.
- **Starfish feed on mollusks and crustaceans. In some areas,** they are a serious threat to oyster and clam beds.
- **Starfish have eyespots at the tip of each** arm. These act as light sensors, and contain a red pigment which changes chemically in the presence of light. They are believed to influence the starfish's behavior, particularly movement.

- **The female anglerfishis six times larger than her mate.** The male anchors himself to the top of her head and stays there for the rest of his life. They literally become one. Their digestive and circulatory systems are merged. Except for to very large generative organs and a few fins, nothing remains of the male.

- **The killer whale, or orca,is not a whale,** but the largest member of the dolphin family.

- **The female condor lays a single egg** once every two years.
- **The female green turtle** sheds tears as she lays eggs on the beach. This washes sand particles out of her eyes and rids her body of excess salt.
- **Studies show that breeds** of dogs that bite the least are, in order: the Golden Retriever, Labrador Retriever, Shetland Sheepdog, Old English Sheepdog and the Welsh Terrier.

- **Sue, the world's largest**, most complete, and best preserved Tyrannosaurus Rex, made her grand debut to the public on 17 May 2000, at the Field Museum in Chicago, Illinois.
- **The female meadow vole** can start reproducing when she is only 25 days old and gives birth to 16 litters per year.
- **The female knot-tying** weaverbird will refuse with a male who has built a shoddy nest. If spurned, the male must take the nest apart and completely rebuild it in order to win the affections of the female.
- **The kinkajou's tail is twice** as long as its body. Every night, it wraps itself up in its tail and uses it as a pillow.
- **Taranto that are seen** wandering around in the wild not make good pets. These are sexually mature males at the end of their life cycle-they will die within a week or months.
- **The female salamander inseminates** herself. At mating time, the male deposits a conical mass of a jellylike substance containing the sperm. The female draws the jelly to herself, and is so doing, fertilizes her eggs.
- **The fennec fox is the** smallest wild dog alive today. At birth the fennec weighs two pounds (0.8 kilograms 0 and will weigh three pounds (1.5 kilograms) in adulthood.
- **The large hind feet of the chinchilla help** it hop like a kangaroo, and its small front legs and feet are similar to those of a squirrel.

- **The largest great white shark ever caught measured 37 feet** and weighed 24,000 pounds. It was found in a herring weir in New Brunswick in 1930.
- **The harmless whale shark holds the title** of largest fish, with the record being a 59-footer captured in Thailand in 1919.
- **The first dinosaur to be found and recognized** as a huge reptile was the Megalosaurus. This dinosaur was a meat eater.

- **The Adele penguin bears the name of French explorer** Dumont d'Urville's beloved wife.
- **The first drawing of a North American swallow tail was** of a male tiger swallowtail. It was drawn in 1587 by John White, commander of Sir Walter Raleigh's third expedition to North America.
- **The African eagle, swooping at more than 100 miles per hour**, can brake to a halt in 20 feet.
- **The first flying animals were the pterosaurs that** appeared over 200 million years ago. They were closer to flying reptiles than birds.

- **The first Komodo dragons to breed in the western world are at the National Zoo at the** Smithsonian Institute in Washington, DC.
- **The American lungfish can live without water for up to four years. When a drought** occurs, it digs a pit and encloses itself in a capsule of slime and earth, leaving a small opening for breathing.

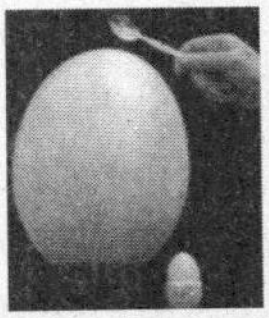

- **The largest known egg ever laid by a creature was that of** the extinct Aepyornis of Madagascar. The egg was 9.5 inches long. It had a volume of 2.35 gallons.

- **The Alaskan moose is the largest deer of the** New World. It attains a height at the withers in excess of seven feet and, when fully grown, weighs up to 1,800 pounds.
- **The largest order of mammals, with about 1,700 species,** is rodents. Bats are second with about 950 specie.
- **The albatross drinks sea water. It has a special desalinization apparatus** that strains out and excretes all excess salt.
- **The last wolf in Great Britain was killed in Scotland, in 1743.** Wolves were extinct in England by 1500.

- **The flying fish builds up speed in the water then leaps into the** air to escape predators. Once in the air, it can stay airborne for up to 325 feet (100m).
- **The flying snake of Java and Malaysia is able to flatten** itself out like a ribbon and sail like a glider from tree to tree.

- **The American opossum, a marsupial, bears its young** just 12 to 13 days after conception.
- **The fur of the vicuna, a small member of the camel family** which lives in the Andes Mountains of Peru, is so fine that each hair is less than two-thousands of an inch. The animal was considered sacred by the Incas, and only royalty could wear its fleece.

- **The American woodcock, with its eyes placed towards the** top of its head, can see backward and upward, and forward and upward, with binocular vision and, laterally, almost 180 degrees with each eye.
- **The gait of the giraffe is a pace, with both legs on one side** moving together. Because of its long stride, a giraffe is quicker than it appears. The animal, at full gallop, can run about 30 miles per hour.
- **The anaconda, one of the world's largest snakes, fives birth to its** young instead of laying eggs.
- **The lethal Lion's Mane jellyfish has a bell reaching up to eight feet** in diameter, and tentacles longer than a blue whale up to 200 feet long. Juveniles are pink, turning red as they mature, and then becoming brownish purple when adults.

- **The ancient nautilus is considered the most intelligent of** the invertebrates; it is said to have been as intelligent as a young cat.
- **The anteater hasn't any teeth or jaws**. Its sticky tongue measures over a foot long.

- **The longest fish is the oarfish, which is shaped like an eel.** On average, it grows to over 20 feet (six meters) in length, but oarfish of 46 feet (14 meters) have been found.
- **The gecko lizard can run on the ceiling without falling** because its toes have flaps of skin that act like suction cups.
- **The antlers of a male moose can have as many** as 30 tines, or spikes.
- **The longest lizard in the world is the Komodo dragon** at 10 feet long. Next is the water monitor at 8.8 feet, then the perenty at 7.8 feet, the common iguana at five feet and the marine iguana at five feet.

- **The antlers of a moose are created from living** tissue supplied by blood through a network of vessels covered with a soft smooth skin called velvet. Eventually the tissue becomes solidified the velvet is scraped off, and the antlers become completely formed of dead matter.
- **The male argues pheasant of Asia has the longest feathers of** all flying birds. Its tails feathers can reach a length of six feet (1.7metres).
- **The male house wren builds several nests as part of his** courtship ritual. Once the nests are completed, his potential bride looks them all over, and then selects one as her preferred choice for the laying of her eggs.
- **The male moose sheds its antlers every winter and** grows a new set the following year.
- **The giant armadillo has as many as 100 teeth**, although they are small and fragile.

- **The giant Pacific octopus can fit its entire body through** an opening no bigger than the size of its beak.
- **The giant squid is the largest creature without a backbone. It weighs** up to 2.5 tons and grows up to 55 feet long. Each eye is a foot or more in diameter.
- **The Gila monster spends about 96 per cent** of its life underground.

- **There are fewer than 1,000 Bactrian camels left in** the wild. They have survived in a land with no water in an area used for nuclear testing. Their numbers, however, are falling dramatically as humans encroach farther and farther into China's Gobi Desert.
- **There are fewer than 1,000 giant pandas** left alive in the world.
- **The massive skeleton of the African elephant accounts for about 15 per cent** of the body weight, just as in a man of slender build; however, the elephant's skeleton supports as much as four tons per leg, and is thus stressed close to the physical limit for bone. To keep from damaging its skeleton, an African elephant has to move sedately, never jumping or running. The 'charge' of these animals is a fast walk on long legs, at about 15 miles per hour.

- **The girth of the Gila monster lizard's tail may shrink by** 80 per cent during times of low food supply.
- **The glue of a barnacle cannot be dissolved with strong** acids or temperatures set as high as 440° F.
- **The minuscule krill shrimp has** eleven pairs of legs.

- **There are more caribou in** Alaska than people.
- **There are more goats than cows in mountainous countries since goats can** survive well by eating grass and other brush.
- **The Mola Mola, or Ocean Sunfish, lays up** to 5 million eggs at one time.

- **The more that is learned about the ecological benefits** of bats, the more home gardeners are going out of their way to entice these amazing winged mammals into their neighbor hoods. Bats are voracious insect eaters, devouring as many as 600 bugs per hour for four to six hours a night. They can eat from one-half to three-quarters their weight per evening.

- **The grey whale, a baleen whale, has a series of up to 180 fringed overlapping** plates hanging from each side of its upper jaw. This is where teeth would be located.

- **The grey wolf is the largest wild dog alive today. As an adult a grey wolf** can weigh up to 176 pounds (80 kilograms).
- **Americans spend more than 5.4 billion dollars on** their pets each year.
- **The great distance between the eyes and nostrils of the hammerhead shark may** allow the animal to detect its prey's direction more accurately. Then are experts at catching the stingrays on which they feed.
- **With nearly 11 million horses owl can** turn its head 270 degrees.

- **The mudskipper is a fish** that can actually walk on land.
- **The grebe, an aquatic bird, has an effective means of** escaping danger while protecting its young. At the first sign of danger, it will sink into the water until its back is level with the surface. This allows its offspring to swim over and quickly climb on to its back. The parent grebe than rises up t its swimming position and ferries the chicks across the water to safety.
- **The musk ox has the longest hair of any polar animal.** The hairs of the outer layer of their coats can reach up to three feet (one metre) long.
- **The nearly 1,000 kinds of bats account for almost a** quarter of all mammal species, and most are highly beneficial.

- **The groundhog is a member of the rodent family. The typical adult groundhog can** weigh approximately eight to 14 pounds and average about 22 inches in length.
- **The nematode Caenorhabditis elegans age the equivalent of five human years for**

every day they live, usually expiring after 14 days. However, when stressed, the worm goes into a state of suspended animation that can last for two months or more. The human equivalent would be to sleep for about 200 years.

- **The gurnard, a fish found in Florida, grunts** when a thunderstorm is brewing, and it's said to be more reliable than meteorologists.
- **There are seven distinctive types of combs on chickens: rose, strawberry,** single, cushion, buttercup, pea and V-shaped.
- **The nest of the African Grey Parrot is a hole in a large** tree. The bird uses no nesting material. It lays its eggs in the wood dust at the bottom of the nest-holes, which are about two to six feet deep (60 to 200cm).

- **There are some 50 different species of sea snakes, and all of them are** venomous. They thrive in abundance along the coast from the Persian Gulf to Japan and around Australia and Melanesia. Their venom is 10 times as virulent as that of the cobra. Humans bitten by them have died within two-and-a-half hours.

- **The New Guinea singing dog's most unique characteristic is its dramatic ability** to vary the pitch of its howl. The animal does not bark repetitively but has a complex vocal behavior, including yelps, whines and single-note howls.
- **The Nile crocodile averages about 45 years in the wild**, and may live up to 80 years of captivity.
- **The hides of mature female blue sharks are more than twice** as thick as those of males, probably as a protection against courtship bites.
- **The now-extinct ancestor of the horse, eohippus, had a short neck,** a pug muzzle and stood no higher than a medium-sized dog.

- **The nurse shark spends much of its time in caves. It leaves the security** of its cave to feed on prey such as lobsters, squid and crabs. The sucking sound of its powerful throat muscles is probably the origin of the animal's common name.

- **There is no single cat called the panther. The name is commonly applied to the leopard, but** it is also used to refer to the puma and the jaguar. A black panther is really a black leopard.
- **The Hirudo leech has three jaws with 100 teeth** on each jaw-making 300 teeth in all.

- **The Amazon leech uses a different method of sucking blood. They insert a** long proboscis into the victim as opposed to biting.
- **There were two main types of dinosaurs: Saurischia dinosaurs had** hip and pelvic bones like lizards and consisted of meat-and plant-eating dinosaurs. Ornithischia dinosaurs had hip and pelvic bones like birds and consisted of small plant-eaters.
- **There were about 60 million bison when the European landed in** America. By the 1880s, all but 500 bison were killed. Today there are 350,000 bison in America.

- **The optimum depth of water in a birdbath is two-and-a-half** inches. Less water makes it difficult for birds to take a bath; more makes them afraid.
- **The Hirudo leech lays its babies within a cocoon; the Amazon leech carries** its babies on its stomach – sometimes as many as 300.
- **The Honduran white bat is snow white with a yellow nose and** ears. It cuts large leaves to make 'tents' that protect its small colonies from jungle rains.

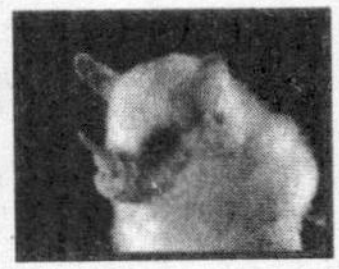

- **The horned lizard of the American southwest may squirt a thin** stream of blood from the corners of its eyes when frightened.
- **The howler monkey is the loudest animal living in the rainforests of South** America. Their voices can be heard up to five miles (eight kilometers) away.

- **Though the Connecticut warbler passes through Connecticut only on its autumn** migration, this shy, seldom-seen songbird bears the name of the state where it was first collected by pioneer ornithologist Alexander Wilson in 1812.
- **The Ozark blind salamander begins life with eyes and plume like** gills. As the animal matures, its eyelids fuse together and the gills disappear.
- **To a human, one giant octopus looks virtually the same** as any other of the same size and species. This explains why divers claim to have seen the same octopus occupy a den for ten or more years. But an octopus seldom lives longer than four years.

- **The pallid bat of western North America is immune to the** stings of scorpions as well as the seven-inch centipedes upon which it feeds.
- **The safeguard its food when away, the wolverine marks it with** a strong musk so foul smelling that other animals won't touch it.
- **The penculine titmouse of Africa builds its home in such a sturdy manner** that Masai tribesman use their nests for purses and carrying cases.

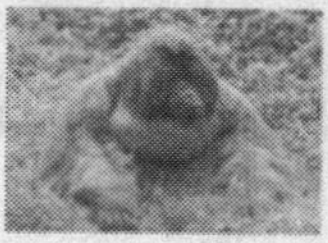

- **To warn off other males, the orangutans of South-east Asia** burp loudly to declare their territory.
- **Pichiciego is a little-known burrowing South America animal that is related** to the armadillo, but is smaller in size. The ending of the animal's name is derived from the Spanish *ciego*, meaning 'blind.'

- **The pigmy shrew—a relative of the mole – is the smallest mammal in North** America. It weighs 1/14 ounce – less than a 5p piece.

- **Today's oldest form of horse is the Przewalski, or Mongolian Wild Horse. Survivors of** this breed were discovered in the Gobi Desert in 1881.
- **The pistol shrimp makes a noise so** loud that it can shatter glass.

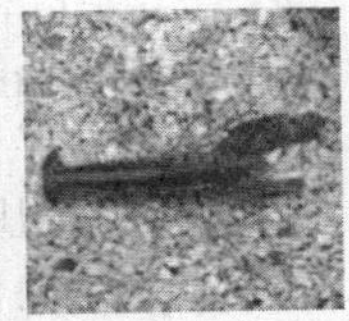

- **Travelling at a rate of two to three miles per** hour, camels can carry 500 to 1,000 pounds on their backs. They are able to keep up this pace for six or seven hours a day. Camels will refuse to carry loads that are not properly balanced.
- **The pitohui bird of Papua New Guinea has enough poison in its** feathers and skin to kill mice and frogs. The poison can affect humans, often causing them numbness, burning and sneezing.

- **Tuna swim at a steady rate of nine miles per hour for** an indefinite period of time – and they never stop moving. Estimates indicate that a 15-year-old tuna travels one million miles in its lifetime.
- **The Portuguese man-of-war is found most commonly in the Gulf Stream of** the northern Atlantic Ocean and in the tropical and subtropical regions of the Indian and Pacific Oceans. It is sometimes found floating in groups numbering in the thousands.

- **The prescribed diet of the Polish Lowland Sheepdog in present-day** Poland consists of bread, potatoes, cottage cheese, milk and an occasional egg.

- **The pronghorn antelope can run at up to 61** miles per hour.

- **Unlike most fish, electric eels cannot get enough** oxygen from water. Approximately every five minutes, they must surface to breathe or they will drown. Unlike most fish, they can swim both backwards and forwards.
- **The quahog, a marine clam, can live for up to 200 years**, making it the longest living ocean creature in the world. Second place goes to the killer whale at 90 years; third is the blue whale at 80 years; fourth is the sea turtle at 50 years; and fifth is the tiger shark at 40 years.

- **The raccoon drives its name from the Indian word** meaning 'he who scratches with his hands'.
- **The rare Hawaiian monk seal has been known to** dive to about 1,650 feet (500m). The animal doesn't 'bark' like sea lions, but has a number of different vocalizations that it produces, including a deep, guttural call that sounds much like a belch.
- **Unlike other reptiles, female alligators protect their young for up to two** years after hatching.
- **The acorn woodpecker leaves its food sticking out of the holes it's drilled in oak trees,** making it easy for squirrels and jays to help themselves.
- **Unrelated to the chicken, the male cock-of–the-rock bird** earned the name 'cock' because of its rooster-like appearance and combative behavior. The female of the species influenced the word 'rock' being added to the name because of her habit of nesting and rearing the young in sheltered rock niches.

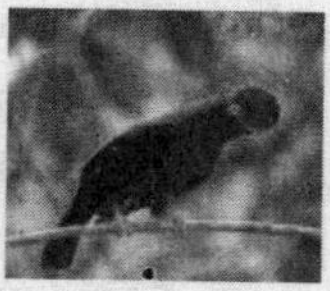

- **Until they were imported into the** country, Australia did not have any members of the cat family, hoofed animals, apes or monkeys.

Religion

- **A young shepherd boy** discovered the Dead Sea Scrolls at Qumran, Jordan, in 1947.
- **Christianity has over a** billion followers. Islam is next in representation with half this number.
- **Kerimaki Church in Finland** is the world's biggest church made of wood.

- **There are more than 1,700 references** to gems and precious stones in the King James version of the Bible.
- **Though Buddhism was founded in India** around 470 BC and developed there at an early date, it was uprooted from India between the seventh and twelfth centuries AD and today exists almost exclusively outside the country, primarily in Sri Lanka, Japan and Indo-China.
- **According to ceremonial customs of** Orthodox Judaism, it is officially sundown when you cannot tell the difference between a black thread and a red thread.
- **George Fox founded** the religious group 'The Quakers'.
- **Martin Luther posted 95 theses** on the Church at Wittenberg in 1517.
- **The members of the Church of** Jesus Christ of Latter Day Saints are better known as 'MORMONS'.
- **The Jewish Sabbath** begins at Sunset on Friday.
- **A muslim who has made a** pilgrimage to Mecca is called Hajji.
- **A winged lion is usually** associated with St. Mark.

Entertainment Arena

- **According to Pope** Innocent III, it was not a crime to kill someone after a game of chess.
- **The total number** of bridge hands possible is 54 octillions.

- ***Abbey Road* was** the last album recorded by the Beatles.
- **Glass flutes do not** expand with humidity so their owners are spared the nuisance of tuning them.
- **The Academy Award** statue is named after a librarian's uncle. One day Margaret Herrick, librarian for the Academy of Motion Picture Arts and Sciences, made the remark that the statue looked her uncle Oscar, and the name stuck.
- **In every show that** Tom Jones and Harvey Schmidt (The Fantasticks) did there was at least one song about rain.
- **The licence plate number** that appears on the Volkswagon that appeared on the cover of the Beatles' *Abbey Road* album was 281 F.

- **Matt Groening, creator of *The Simpsons*, incorporated** his initials into the drawing of Homer. M is his hair and G is his ear.
- **On the cartoon show *The Jetsons*, Jane is 33 years** old and her daughter Judy is 18.
- **The Looney Tunes song is actually called** 'the merry-go-round is broken down'.

- **Tweety used to be a baby bird without feathers** until the censors made him have feathers because he looked naked.
- **Wilma Flintstone's maiden name was Wilma Slaghoopal, and Betty Rubble's was Betty** Jean Mcbricker.

- **Since the Lego Group began manufacturing blocks in 1949,** more than 189 billion pieces in 2000 different shapes have been produced. This is enough for about 30 Lego pieces for every living person on earth.
- **The Ouija board is named after the French and** German words for yes – *oui* and *ja*.
- **Westwood Studious' computer game 'Command and Conquer' is** the most successful war game series of all time according to the *Guinness Book of World Records*.
- **Four people played Darth Vader: David Prowse** was his body, James Earl Jones did the voice, Sebastian Shaw was his face and a fourth person did the breathing.

- **In Disney's *Fantasia*, the sorcerer's name** is Yensid (Disney spelled backwards).
- **In Psycho, the colour of Mrs. Bates's** dress was periwinkle blue.
- **In the *Return of the Jedi* special edition during the new** Couruscant footage at the end of the film a stormtrooper can be seen being carried over the crowds.

- **In the 1983 film *JAWS 3D* the shark blows up. Some of** the shark guts were stuffed ET dolls being sold at the time.
- **In the film 'Star Trek: First Contact', when Picard shows Lilly she is** orbiting earth, Australia and Papua New Guinea are clearly visible... but New Zealand is missing.
- **In the *Mario Brothers* movie, the Princess's first name is Daisy,** but in Mario 64, the game, her first name is Peach. Before that, it's Princess Toadstool.

- **In the movie *'Now and Then'*, when the girls are** taking to the hippie (Brendan Fraser) and they get up to leave, Teeny (Thora Birch) puts out her cigarette twice.
- **Luke Skywalker's last name was changed at the** last minute from Starkiller in order to make it less violent.
- **Skull island is the jungle home** of King Kong.

- **The famous theme ostensibly from *'Dragnet'* was actually composed by** Miklos Rozsa for the 1946 film noir classic *The Killers*.
- **The first real motion picture theatre was called** a Nickelodeon (admission was a nickel) and opened in McKeesport Pennsylvania near Pittsburg. The first motion picture shown there was *The Great Train Robbery*.
- **The movie Clue has three different endings. Each ending was** randomly chosen for different theatres. All three endings are present in the home video.

- **The name of Jabba the Hut's** pet spider monkey is Salacious Crumb.
- **The name of the dog from** *The Grinch Who Stole Christmas* was Max.
- **The second unit films movie shots that do not require the** presence of actors.
- **The skyscraper in *Die Hard* is the** Century Fox Tower.
- **Aerosmith's 'Dude looks like a lady,'** was written about Vince Neil of Motley Crue.

- **Don MacLean's song 'American Pie' was written about Buddy Holly, The** Big Bopper and Richie Valens. All three were on the same plane that crashed.
- **In 1976, Rodrigo's 'Guitar Concierto de Aranjuez' was No 1 in** the UK for only three hours because of a computer error.
- **20252 is Smokey the Bear's own** zip code.
- **Approximately 60 circus performers have been shot from cannons.** At last report, 31 of these have been killed.

- **Boris Karloff is the narrator of the seasonal** television special *How the Grinch Stole Christmas.*
- **Bret Hart trademarked** the nickname 'Hitman' in 1990.
- **Carnegie Mellon University offers bag** piping as a major.
- **In 1938, Joe Shuster and Jerry Siegel sold all rights** to the comic-strip character Superman to their publishers for $130.

- **Kermit the Frog has 11 points** to his collar around his neck.
- **Kermit the Frog** is left-handed.

- **Steely Dan got their name form a *sexual* device depicted in** the book *The Naked Lunch.*
- **The average British family views television** six hours each day.
- **The music hall entertainer Nosmo King derived his stage mane** from a 'No Smoking' sign.
- **There are Pokemon school** books. You can even do maths with a Pokemon maths book.
- **In 1990, there were an estimated 75,000** accordionists in the United States.

- **Jonathan Houseman Davis, lead singer of Korn**, was born a Presbyterian, but converted to Catholicism because his mother wanted to marry his stepfather in a Catholic church.

- **The 80s song 'Rosanna' was written** by Rosanna Arquette, the actress.
- **The B52s, were named after** a fifties hairdo.
- **The Grateful Dead were once called** 'The Warlocks'.
- **The Mamas and Papas were once** called the Mugwumps.

- **The only member of the band ZZ Top to not** have a beard has the last name Beard.
- **There is a music band named** 'A Life-Threatening Buttocks Condition'.

- **The song with the longest title is 'I'm a Cranky Old Yank in** a Clanky Old Tank on the Streets of Yokohama with my Honolulu Mama Doin' Those Beat-o, Beat-o Flat –On-My-Seat-o, Hirohito Blues' written by Hoagy Carmichael. He later claimed the song title ended with 'Yank' and the rest was a joke.

- **Tommy James was in a New York hotel looking at the Mutual of New** York building's neon sign flashing repeatedly: M-O-N-Y. He suddenly got the inspiration to write his #1 hit 'Mony Mony'.
- **'When I'm Sixty-Four' was the first song to be recorded for the** *Sgt. Pepper* album. 'Within You without You' was the last.
- **Caruso and Roy Orbison were the only** tenors this century capable of hitting 'e' over high 'c'.
- **One in every four Americans** has appeared on television.
- **60.2 per cent of the US TV audience** watched the final episode of *M*A*S*H* in 1983.
- **As well as appearing in *Star Trek*,** William Shatner, Leonard Nimoy, James Doohan and George Takei have all appeared at one time or another on *The Twilight Zone.*

- **Captain Jean-Luc Picard's** fish was named Livingston.
- **Daytime dramas are called soap operas because they were** originally used to advertise soap powder. In America in the early days of TV, advertises would write stories around the use of their soap powder.

- **For many years, the globe on the *NBC Nightly News*** spun in the wrong direction. On 2 January 1984, NBC finally set the world spinning back in the proper direction.

- **In *Gilligan's Island*, the Professor's real name was Roy Hinkley, Mary Ann's** last name was Summers and Mrs. Howell's maiden name was Wentworth.

- **In every episode of *Seinfeld* there** is a Superman somewhere.
- **In the theme song from *The Flintstones*, the** line after 'Let's ride with the family down the street' is 'through the courtesy of Fred's two feet!'
- **Jamie Farr (who played Klinger on Mash) was the only member of** the cast who actually served as a soldier in the Korean War.

- **Mr. Munster's first** name is Herman.
- **Mr. Spock was second in command** of the Starship Enterprise.
- **My Spock's blood type was** T-Negative.
- **On the Roseanne show, DJ stood for** David Jacob.
- **TV sitcom characters rarely say goodbye when** they hang up the phone.
- **The actor who played Wedge in the** original *Star Wars* trilogy has a famous nephew: actor Ewan McGregor, who plays young Obi-Wan in the new Star Wars film.
- **The Brady Brunch went to elementary school at** Dixie Canyon Elementary.

- **The character Bert and Ernie on *Sesame Street*** were named after Bert the cop and Ernie the taxi driver in Frank Capra's *It's a Wonderful Life.*
- **The first crime mentioned in the first episode of** *Hill Street* blues was armed robbery.

- **The first ever televised murder case appeared on** TV in 1955, 5-9 December. The accused was Harry Washburn.
- **The name of the 'Love Boat'** was the *Pacific Princess.*
- **The wheel on the game show** *'Wheel of Fortune'* is 102 inches in diameter.
- **There are as many as 78** scenes in a single *X-Files* episode.

- **TV's top-rated series** from 1957 to 1961 was *Gunsmoke.*
- **'Video Killed the Radio Star' was the** very first video ever played on MTV.
- **The world-renowned scientist who** played himself in an episode of *Star Trek: The Next Generation* was Stephen Hawking.
- **John Travalto played the inept** hit man Vincent Vega in the film *Pulp Fiction.*
- **The cartoon character who said** *'Yabadabadoo'* is Fred Flinstone.
- **Bengal's Sherlock Holmes** is Bomkesh Bakshi.
- **Paul McCarthney wrote** 'Hey Jude' for Julian Lenon.

Food and Drink

- **Blueberry Jelly Bellies** were created especially for Ronald Reagan.
- **Honey is used as** a centre for golf balls and in antifreeze mixtures.
- **In the summer**, walnuts get a tan.
- **Mexican jumping beans** jump because of a moth larva inside the bean.
- **Pepsi is commonly used** by wooden boat owners to clean mould from decks. You can spill it on for about 30 seconds, but it needs rinsing to make sure it does not erode your decks completely.
- **Rice is grown on more than** 10 per cent of the earth's farmable surface.
- **Saturday night is the** biggest night of the week for eating pizza.
- **Shredded Wheat was** the first ready-to-eat breakfast cereal.
- **The average 190 sticks** of gum, drinks 600 sodas and 800 gallons of water, eats 135 pounds of sugar and 19 pounds of cereal per year.

- **The colour of a chili** is no indication of its spiciness, but size usually is – the smaller the pepper, the hotter it is.
- **The dark meat on** a roast turkey has more calories than the white meat.

- **The highest lifetime** yield of milk for a single cow is 465,224 lbs.
- **There is no such thing** as blue food, even blueberries are purple.
- **Widows of a recently** deceased king among the Baganda people of Uganda, have the honour of drinking the beer in which the king's entrails have been cleaned.
- **Ray Kroc bought McDonalds** for $2.7 million in 1961 from the McDonald brothers.
- **The most common pear** world-wide is the Bartlett. It is bell-shaped, sweet and soft with a light green colour.

- **'Tomatina' is the legendary** Spanish tomato-throwing festival.
- **It's impossible to get** water out of a rimless tyre.
- **The dried buds of a tree** of the myrtle family are called *cloves*.
- ***Sashimi* is Japanese** raw fish.
- **The drink made from** 'fermented pear juice' is called *Perry*.
- **'A timbale' is a small round** mould or food cooked in one.
- **'En papillote' is the French term** to describe ffod cooked and wrapped in paper.
- **A cocktail made from** bourbon, bitters, sugar and fruit is called 'Old Fashioned'.
- **Another name for the** 'kiwi fruit' is 'Chinese gooseberry'.
- **The British call it 'candy floss';** the Americans call it 'cotton floss'.
- **Vodka is made from** fermented grain of potatoes.
- **Salt beef, seasoned and smoked** is called 'pastrami'.
- **A welsh tea bread** is called 'bara brith'.
- **The American call** 'cornflower' – 'corn starch'.

History

- **Each king in a deck** of playing cards represents a great king from history: spades—King David; clubs—Alexander the Great; hearts—Charlemagne; diamonds—Julius Caesar.

- **The only painting Vincent van Gogh** sold in his lifetime was the Red Vineyard.
- **The Roman emperor Nero** "married" his male slave Scotus.
- **King Kong was** Adolph Hitler's favorite movie.
- **Nazi leader Adolph Hitler** had only one testicle.
- **Leonardo da Vinci** was dyslexic, and he often wrote backwards.
- **Marie Curie, the Nobel prize** winning scientist who discovered radium, died of radiation poisoning.
- **In 1897, Bayer**, who is the maker of Aspirin, marketed the drug heroin
- **In 1998, Sony accidentally** sold 700,000 camcorders that had the technology to see through people's clothes.
- **Michelangelo's cook was** illiterate, so he drew her a shopping list—which today is priceless.
- **Spiral staircases in medieval** castles ran clockwise so that attacking knights climbing the stairs couldn't use their right hands—their sword hands—while the defending knights coming down could. And left-handed men, believed to descend from the devil, couldn't become knights.

- **The shortest war in** history was between Zanzibar and England in 1896: Zanzibar surrendered after thirty-eight minutes.
- **Pirates wore earrings** in the belief that it improved their eyesight.
- **The architect who built** the Kremlin had his eyes gouged out by Ivan the Terrible so that he'd never be able to design another building like it.
- **In ancient Egypt, priests** plucked every hair from their bodies, including their eyebrows and eyelashes.
- **U.S. presidents** John F. Kennedy and Warren Harding were both survived by their fathers.

- **Adolf Hitler's mother** seriously considered having an abortion but was talked out of it by her doctor:
- **Cleopatra wrote a book** on cosmetics. One of the ingredients was burned mice.
- **The first country to** abolish capital punishment was Austria, in 1787.
- **Richard the Lion Heart** spent just four months of his life in England.
- **Leonardo da Vinci** could write with one hand and draw with the other at the same time.

Things That Started in the 1950s

- **Rock 'n' roll, nuclear** submarines, credit cards, NATO, the miss world contest, this Is your life, tea bags, the Frisbee, tranquilisers, Disneyland, the Guinness Book of records, space travel, Lego, transistor hearing aids, Cinemascope, diet soft drinks (no-cal ginger ale),the yellow pages, Barbie dolls, automatic electric kettles, heart pacemakers, type-writer correction fluid, microwave ovens, Velcro, nonstick saucepans, the Moonies, polio vaccines, Beatniks, kidney transplants, roll-on deodorants, boutiques, disposable diapers.

- **A B-25 bomber airplane** crashed into the 79th floor of the Empire State Building on 28 July, 1945.
- **A golden razor removed** from King Tut's tomb was still sharp enough to be used.
- **Acting was once considered** evil, and actors in the first English play to be performed in America were arrested.
- **All office seekers** in the Roman Empire were obliged to wear a certain white toga for a period of one year before the election.
- **At the turn of the** last millennium, Dublin had the largest slave market in the world, run by the Vikings.
- **Shankaracharya was** responsible for the revival of Brahmanical Hinduism.
- **In 1954, boxers and wrestlers** had to swear under oath they were not communists before they could compete in the state of Indiana.
- **Dinner guests during** the medieval times in England were expected to bring their own knives to the table.
- **During the Depression**, banks first used cellotape to mend torn currency.
- **The term 'Vedas' in** Sanskrit literally means 'knowledge'.
- **During the Middle Ages**, few people were able to read or write. The clergy were virtually the only ones that could.
- **During the Middle Ages**, it was widely believed that men had one less rib than women. This is because of the story in the Bible that Eve had been created out of Adam's rib.
- **Manu Smriti is** also known as the 'Laws of Manu'.
- **Evidence of shoemaking** exists as early as 10,000 BC.
- **In 1900, the third** leading cause of death was diarrhea.
- **The epic *Mahabharata*** was originally known as Jaya.
- **In ancient Egypt**, killing a cat was a crime punishable by death.
- **In certain parts of India** and ancient China mouse meat was considered a delicacy.

- **In medieval England**, beer was often served with breakfast.
- **Income tax was first** introduced in England in 1799 by British Prime Minister William Pitt.
- **Morocco was the first** country to recognize the United States in 1789.
- **New Zealand was the first** country to give women the vote in 1890.
- **Pilgrims ate popcorn** at the first thanks giving dinner.
- **Bheeshma literally means** 'a man of terrible oath'.
- **The origin of the most** used four-letter word: in Irish police Stations in the 19th century – when public indecency was a serious crime – couples were charged with being Found Under Carnal Knowledge.
- **The hundred years** war lasted for 116 years.
- **The Japanese anthem** has the oldest lyrics/text from the ninth century, but the music is from 1880.
- **The Noble prize** was first awarded in 1901.
- **Vikings use the** skulls of their enemies as drinking vessels.
- **Samyag Darshan**, Samyag Gyan, Samyag Charitra are known as the 3 jewels of Jainism.

- **Sangam literature** indicates the Chola Dynasty antedated 100 CE.
- **Panini was the father** of Sanskrit grammar.
- **The Spanish Civil War last** for three years in 1930s.
- **The great event that took place** in 1851 was 'The Great Exhibition'.
- **The dynasty that ruled Russia** for over 300 years was the RAMANOV dynasty.
- **The American general who was** known as 'Old Blood and Guts' was General George Patton.
- **The oldest man to become a** US president was Ronald Reagan.

Literary World

The Written Word

- **Euclid is** the most successful textbook writer of all time. His *Elements,* written around 300 B.C., has gone through more than 1,000 editions since the invention of printing.
- **Virgil,** who is generally accepted as the greatest of the Roman poets, left instructions that, upon his death, his manuscript of the *Aeneid* should be burned because he had not been able to polish it. Roman emperor Augustus—who may have been the one who requested Virgil to write it—stepped in and countermanded Virgil's request. He had others polish the work, and ordered it published.
- **Paper** was invented in China around 105 A.D., by the eunuch Ts'ai Lun.
- **The story of Cinderella** first appears in a Chinese book written in the 850s.
- **Shakespeare used** around 29,000 different words in his plays. About 10,000 of those words had never previously been used in any surviving English literature. Around 6,000 words only appear once.
- **Over 2,500,000,000 copies** of the Bible have been made.
- **Agatha Christie** is the top-selling English-language author of all time. She wrote 78 mystery novels that have sold an estimated 2,000,000,000 copies
- **The Guinness Book of World Records**, first published in 1955, got into itself nineteen years later, in 1974, by setting a record as the fastest-selling book in the world.

- **Shakespeare's most talkative character** is Hamlet, who has 1,422 lines in Hamlet. None of his other characters have as many lines in a single play.
- **The largest book in the world**, a copy of the *Tripitaka*, the sacred Buddhist text that includes Buddha's teachings, is inscribed on 729 marble slabs, each 3.5' × 5' × 5", and occupies a thirteen-acre site on the grounds of the Kuthodaw pagoda in Mandalay, Burma.
- **Virginia Woolfe wrote** all her books standing up.
- **Emily Dickinson wrote** over 1,800 poems. Only seven were published in her lifetime, all without her consent.
- **Anachronisms: Shakespeare** makes Lear, an early Anglo-Saxon King, speak of not wanting spectacles. In relating Macbeth's death, in 1054, and King John's reign in 1200, he mentions cannons. In Julius Caesar, he makes the clock strike three. However, these three inventions were not invented until the fourteenth century.

- **Largest bookstore chain**: AH Wheeler & Co (P) Ltd, is the largest bookstore chain in India.
- **Longest epic**: Mahabharata is the longest epic in the world.
- **Most Expensive Indian Book** is "Firefly - A Fairytale", written by famous fashion designer Ritu Beri. The book is priced at Rs 1 lakh and is published by Ritu Beri herself. Famous publisher Penguin had earlier commissioned Ritu Beri to write the book but abandoned the project after hearing the price for the book she had in mind.
- **Longest Indian Novel** is Avakasikal, written by MK Menon in Malayalam under the penname "Vilasini". The novel runs into 3,958 pages in four volumes and took ten years to complete.
- **Virginia Woolf and her husband** in 1917 founded Hogarth Press.

- **General Lew Wallace's** bestseller *Ben Hur* was the first work of fiction to be blessed by a Pope.

- **Guinness Book of Records** holds the record for being the book most often stolen from public libraries.
- **Mary Shelley** wrote Frankenstein at the age of 19.
- **People in Iceland** read more books per capita than any other people in the world.
- **The all-time bestselling electronic book** is Stephen King's *Riding the Bullet.*
- **The Book of Esther** in the Bible is the only book which does not mention the name of God.
- **Tom Sawyer** was the first novel written on a typewriter.
- **A 'prestidigitator'** is another word for magician.
- **A castrated rooster** is called a capon.
- **A conchologist** studies molluses and shells.
- **A deltiologist** collects postcards.
- **A fingerprint** is also known as a dactylogram.
- **A funambulist** is a tightrope walker.
- **A group of bears** is called a sleuth.
- **A group of kittens** is called a kindle.
- **A group of meteorologists** is called a Shower.
- **A gynaephobic** man fears woman.
- **A horologist** measures time.
- **A klazomaniac** is someone who feels like shouting.
- **A librocubicularist** is someone who reads in bed.
- **A loobry** is the collections of magazines in the toilet.
- **A phonophobe** fears noise.
- **A phrenologist** feels and interprets skull features.
- **An anthropophagist** eats people.
- **Carcinomaphobia** is the fear of cancer.
- **A Knight of** the Industry means a thief.
- **Certain sounds in the English language** are real germ spreaders, particularly the sound of F,P,T,D, & S.

- **Nyctohylophobia** is the fear of dark wooded areas, of forests at night.
- **'Driving pigs to the market'** would mean snoring.
- **A Cat's lick** would mean a quick bath.
- **A Soldier's wash** means taking water in your hand to wash your face.
- **Paedophobia** is the fear of children.
- **A brown bag lunch** means carrying one lunch to the office often in an old office brown envelope.
- **Rhythm and syzygy** are the longest English words without vowels.
- **Scuba stands for** 'self-contained underwater breathing apparatus'.
- **Skepticisms** is the longest typed word that alternates hands.

- **Spat–out food** is called chanking.
- **Taphephobia** is the fear of being buried alive.
- **Telephonophobia** is the fear of telephones.
- **The ball on top of a flagpole** is called the truck.
- **A Panhandler is** one who begs.
- **Tea is also** called 'scandal broth'.
- **Onomastications study** origin of names of places and persons.
- **The Aztec language gives** us the word chocolate.
- ***Kichiree* was called** Kedgeree by the Brits in India.
- **The word 'husband' literally** means the master of the house.
- **A group of husbands** is called an Unhappiness.
- **A group of wives** is an Impatience.
- **A group of** ex-wives is called a Pain.
- **French postcards or obscene** pictures are called American postcards in France.

- **The only word in** English that begins and ends with the letters 'und' is underground.
- **An uxoriphobe hates** his wife.
- **A curtain lecture** is nagging by a wife at bed time.
- **A dutch wife** is a bolster.
- **A dutch nightingale** is a frog.
- **A speedbreaker is also** called a 'sleeping policemen'.
- **A man who has 'hollow legs'** means he can drink heavily as the drinks will not go to his head.
- **The fox's tail** is called a brush.

- **Snapping of your fingers is** also called 'butterfly hiccups'.
- **An Australian Salute means** waving your hand across your face to ward away flies.
- **A haliostis** means having bad breath.
- **Grandmother's sister** will be our 'grand aunt'.
- **The 'geography of the house' means** the toilet.
- **An outdoor toilet in** Australia is called a Thunder Box.
- **The letter W** is the only letter in the alphabet that doesn't have one syllable, it has three.
- **The longest word** in the English language is 1909 letters long and it refers to a distinct part of DNA.
- **The meaning of 'stool pigeon'** is an informer or a traitor.
- **The most common letters** in the English language are R, S, T, L, N, and E.
- **The most used letter** in the English alphabet is E, and Q is the least used.
- **The Old English word** for sneeze is *fneosam*.
- **The oldest word** in the English language is *town*.
- **"Lollipop" is the longest word** that can be typed using only the right hand.

- **The letters H, I, O, and X** are the only letters that look the same if you flip them upside down or view them from behind.
- **"Queueing"** is the only word with five consecutive vowels.
- **The only city in the United States whose name** is spelled using only vowels is Aiea, Hawaii.
- **The longest one-syllable words** are "screeched" and "strengths".
- **The word with the most consonants** in a row is "*latchstring*".
- **"Therein" contains ten words** without rearranging any of the letters: there, in, the, he, her, here, ere, therein, herein, rein.
- **A, H, I, M, O, T, U, V, W, X, and Y** are the symmetric capital letters.
- **The symmetric lowercase letters** are i, l, o, t, u, v, w, x.
- **The only contemporary words** that end with *gry* are angry and hungry.
- **"Deeded" is the only word that** is made using only two different letters, each used three times.
- **The only words with three consecutive double letters** are "bookkeeping" and "bookkeeper".
- **"Polish"** changes from a noun or a verb to a nationality when it is capitalized.
- **If you spell out every number from 0 to 999,** you will find every vowel except for "a". You have to count to one thousand to find an "a"!
- **The highest scoring word in the game Scrabble** is "**quartzy**".
- **"Subcontinental" is the only word that** uses each vowel only once and in reverse alphabetical order.
- **The longest English word that contains neither** A, E, I, O, nor U is *rhythms.*
- **In English, the days of the week are named after the Saxon gods** (except for Saturday, which is named after

the Roman god of agriculture). Sunday is named after the sun, Monday after the moon, Tuesday after Tiw, Wednesday after Woden, Thursday after Thor, Friday after Frige, and Saturday after Sa.

- **The word *boycott* comes from** Charles C. Boycott. He was hired by an Irish earl to collect high rents from tenant farmers who completely ignored him.
- **The word "mile" comes from the Roman *milia*, "thousands".** The Romans measured distances in paces, which were about five feet. So, *milia passum*, 1,000 paces or about 5,000 feet, was the length of a mile
- **Part of a Roman soldier's pay was called** *salarium argentium*, "salt money", which was used to buy the then-precious commodity, and so pay today is called a "salary".
- **A group of magpies is called** a tiding.
- **A group of ravens** is an unkindness.
- **A group of** turtledoves a pitying.
- **A group of** of starlings is a murmuration.
- **A group of** swans is a lamentation.
- **A group of** ponies is a string.
- **A group of** rattlesnakes is a rhumba.
- **A group of** crows is a murder.
- **A group of** cobras is a quiver.
- **A group of** foxes is a skulk.
- **A group of** emus is a mob
- **A group of** elks is a gang.
- **A group of** cats is a clowder.
- **A group of** flamingoes is a pat.
- **A group of** bears is a sleuth.
- **Groups of geese are named in a peculiar manner;** when they are on the ground they are called a "gaggle", but in the air they are called a "skein".

- **The word "daisy" comes from the Old English** "daeges eage", meaning "day's eye", as it reminded people of the sun.

- **The word "kindergarten" comes from the German** for "children's garden". Friedrich Froebel, who coined the term, originally was planning to use the term "Kleinkinderbeschäftigungsanstalt" instead.
- **The word "tragedy" is derived** from two Greek words meaning "goat song".
- **The first use of the word "robot"** to describe advanced humanlike machines was in 1920, in *R.U.R.*, an early science fiction play. It comes from the Czech word *robota*, meaning "compulsory labour".
- **The word "abracadabra" originated** in Roman times as part of a prayer to the god Abraxas.

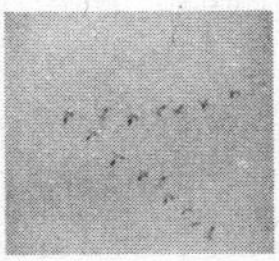

- **The phrase sleep tight originated** when mattresses were set upon ropes woven through the bed frame. To remedy sagging ropes, one would use a bed key to tighten the rope.
- **The term potty** comes from the pintsized chamber pot built for children.
- **The two ends** of a magnet are called poles.
- **The U in U-boats** stands for 'under water'.
- **The word constipation** comes from a Latin word that means 'to crowd together'
- **The word curfew** originates from an old French word that means 'cover fire'.
- **The word diastima** is the word for having a gap between your teeth.
- **The word lethologica** describes the state of not remembering the word you want to say.
- **The word noon** came from an old church term 'none' meaning three. There was a monastic order that would not eat until that time. Since they rang the bells indicating

time, none came earlier and earlier. The towns people called midday noon to ridicule them.

- **The word racecar** and kayak are palindromes: the same whether they are read left to right or right to left.
- **The word rodent** comes from the Latin word *rodere* meaning to gnaw.
- **The word samba** means to rub navels together.
- **The word assassination** and *bump* were invented by Shakespeare.
- **There are only four words** in the English language which end in –dous: *tremendous*, *horrendous*, *stupendous* and *hazardous*.
- **There are only three world** capitals that begin with the letter O in English: Ottawa, Canada; Oslo, Norway; and Ouagadougou, Burkina Faso.
- **There are six words** in the English language with the letter combination uu. Muumuu, Vacuum, continuum, duumvirate, duumvir and residuum.
- **There are 10 body parts** that are only three letters long: eye, ear, leg, arm, jaw, gum, toe, lip, hip and rib.
- **There was no punctuation** until the 15th century.
- **Tonsurphobia** is the fear of haircuts.
- **When two words are combined** to form a single word (e.g. motor + hotel = motel, breakfast + Lunch = brunch) the new word is called a porcelator.
- **Women who wink** at men are known as 'nictitating' women.
- **Xenophobia** is the fear of strangers or foreigners.
- **1961 was the most recent year** that could be written upside-down and right side-up and appear the same. **The next year** that this will be possible will be 6009!
- **2,488,200 books** will be shipped in the next 12 months with the wrong cover.
- **A coward** was originally a boy who took care of cows.
- **A group of crows** is called a murder.

- **A group of officers** is called a mess.
- **A hamlet is a village** without a church and a town is not a city until it has a cathedral.
- **A necropsy** is an autopsy on animals.
- **A poem written to celebrate** a wedding is called a *epithalamium*.
- **A postcard collector** is called a *deltiologist*.
- **A scholar who studies** the Marquis de Sade is called a Sadian not a Sadist.

- **According to Genesis** 1:20 – 22, the chicken came before the egg.
- **All Hebrew originating names** that end with the letters 'ei' have something to do with God.
- **Alma mater** means bountiful mother.
- **An animal epidemic** is called an epizootic.
- **Archibutyrophobia** is the fear of peanut butter sticking to the roof of your mouth.
- **Before the turn of the century, the papers** were called tabloids, chronicles, gazettes, etc. Most had local stories and far away stories were quite old as it took a while for stories to travel (and of course they were subject to changes from hand to hand.) With the event of the teletype, stories could be broadcast all over at unheard of speed. Several of the papers started carrying a section with stories from all over – North, East, West & South and that's why they are called newspapers.
- **Bookkeeper** is the only word in the English language with three consecutive double letters.
- **Chevrolet** tried marketing a Chevrolet Nova in Spanish – speaking countries – it didn't sell well because NO VA means 'doesn't go' in Spanish.
- **Clans long ago** that wanted to get rid of their unwanted people without killing them used to burn down their houses – hence the expression *get fired.*
- **Clinophobia** is the fear of beds.

- **Corduroy** comes from the French, cord du roi or 'cloth of the king'.
- **Degringolade** means to fall and disintegrate.
- **Dendrology** is the study of trees.
- **Dibble** means to drink like a duck.
- **Bernard Shaw** said, "The true artist will let his wife starve, his children go barefoot, his mother drudge for his living at seventy, sooner than work at anything but his art"?
- **Milton**: Milton, the blind poet of 17th century England received the worst publishing deal of all time: 10 pounds for his greatest work of literature, 'Paradise Lost'.
- **Jack Dawkins** was better known by his working name 'The Artful Dodger' and appeared in the novel 'Oliver Twist'.
- **James Bond, 007** according to the films not the books liked his 'Martini shaken, not stirred'.

The Most Valuable Words You can Make at Scrabble

- **Quizzify** — To cause to look odd 31
- **Whipjacka** — Whining beggar who pretends to be a sailor 29
- **Highjack** — Alternative spelling of hijack 28
- **Jumbolze** — To enlarge a ship by adding a prefabricated section 28
- **Beziques** — Plural of card game 28
- **Caziques** — West Indian chiefs 28
- **Quizzery** — Collections of quizzes or information pertaining to quizzes 28
- **Tzaddiqs** — In Judaism, leaders or persons of extraordinary piety 28
- **Vizcacha** — South American burrowing rodent of heavy build 27

- **Zambucks** New Zealand or Australian colloquial term for members of St. John's Ambulance Brigade

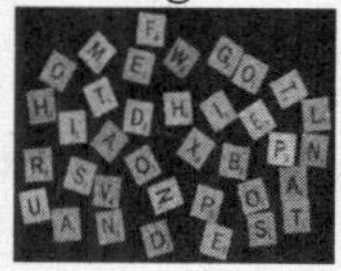

Banned Books

- **The Catcher in the Rye (J. D. Salinger)**: banned in Boron, California, in 1989 because of the word goddamn. This is probably the most famous work of fiction never to have been turned into a feature film.
- **The Adventures of Tom Sawyer (Mark Twain)**: banned by several London libraries (in politically correct Labour-controlled boroughs) in the mid-1980s on account of the book's "racism" and "sexism".
- **Black Beauty (Anna Sewell)**: banned by the African country Namibia in the 1970s because the government took offense at the "racist" title.
- **The Scarlet Pimpernel (Baroness Orczy)**: banned by the Nazis—not because of its language or its theme (though Leslie Howard starred in an anti Nazi film entitled Pimpernel Smith)—but because Baroness Orczy was Jewish. Other authors banned by the Nazis for the same reason included Erich Maria Remarque, Thomas Mann, Sigmund Freud and Marcel Proust.
- **Authors banned by the Nazis** because of their political sentiments included Ernest Hemingway, Upton Sinclair and Jack London.

- **Noddy (Eind Blyton)**: banned by several British libraries in the 1960s—along with other Enid Blyton books—because they weren't thought to be "good" for children.
- **The Grapes of Wrath (John Steinbeck)**: banned from schools in the state of Iowa in 1980 after a parent complained that the classic novel—by the Nobel Prize Winner—was "vulgar and obscene."Steinbeck's other famous novel, of mice and men, has also been banned in other U.S. states for similar reasons.

- **The Joy of Sex (Alex Comfort)**: banned in Ireland from its publication until 1989 on account of the book's uninhibited approach to sex and relationship. The Irish have done more than their share of banning: All of Steinbeck and Zola's novels were banned in Ireland in 1953 for being "subversive" and/ or "immoral". Other books once banned by the Irish include Brave New world (Aldous Huxley), Elmer Gantry (Sinclair Lewis) and The Sun Also Rises (Ernest Hemingway).
- **On the Origin of species (Charles Darwin)**: banned in several U.S. states (especially in the Christian fundamentalist South) through the years – but particularly before World War II—owing to the fact that Darwin didn't accept the Bible's account of Creation. Incredibly, Desmond Morris's The Naked Ape has been banned from one or two U.S. libraries on the same basis. Darwin's book was also banned by the USSR because it was "immoral."
- **In 1898 (14 years prior to the *Titanic* tragedy)**, Morgan Robertson wrote a novel called *Futility*. This fictitious novel was about the largest ship ever built hitting an iceberg in the Atlantic ocean on a cold April night.
- **"Keeping Warm With an Axe" is** the title of a real how-to book.
- **The only person to decline a** Pulitzer Prize for Fiction was Sinclair Lewis for his book *Arrowsmith*.
- **A sultan's wife is** called a sultana.
- **Acrophobia is the** fear of heights.
- **Killing a king is** called regicide.
- **The letter J does not appear** anywhere on the periodic table of elements.
- **A 17th-century Swedish philologist** claimed that in the Garden of Eden God spoke Swedish, Adam spoke Danish and oyster is called a spat.
- **A Flemish artist is responsible** for the world's smallest painting in history. It is a picture of a miller and his mill, and it was painted on to a grain of corn.

- **A hydrodaktulpsychicharmonica** is a variety of musical glass.
- **Arnold Schonberg suffered from triskaidecphobia**, the fear of the number 13. He died 13 minutes form midnight on Friday the 13th.
- **Cleveland spelled backwards** is DNA level C.
- **Dr Seuss coined the word nerd** in his 1950 book *If I Ran The Zoo.*
- **EEG stands for** Electroencephalogram.
- **EMI stands for** 'Electrical and Musical Instrument.
- **Fido means 'faithful'** in Latin.
- **German is considered the** sister language of English.

- **If each count were one** second long, it would take about 12 days to count to a million and 32 years to count to a billion.
- **In Ethiopia, both males and females** of the Surma tribes shave their heads as a mark of beauty.
- **10 October is** National Metric Day.
- **Rio de Janeiro translated** to River of January.
- **The 'you are here arrow'** on a map is called the IDEO locator.
- **The abbreviation for** one pound, lb, comes from the astrological sign Libra meaning balance.
- **The correct response to** the Irish greeting 'Top of the morning to you', is 'And the rest of the day to yourself'.
- **The earliest document in Latin** in a woman's handwriting (it is from the first century AD) is an invitation to a birthday party.

- **The French term 'bourrage de crane'** for wartime propaganda means brain stuffing.

- **The heraldic term 'gules'**, meaning red, comes from the French word gueules, meaning a throat.
- **The infinity character on** the keyboard is called a lemniscate.
- **The longest place name** still in use is: Taumatawhakatangihangaoauauotameteaturipukakapikimaungahoronukupokaiwhenuakitanatahu – a New Zealand hill.
- **The longest place name in Great Britain** is that of a Welsh village.
- **The metal part of a lamp** that surrounds the bulb and supports the shade is called a *harp*.
- **The monastic hours are** matins, lauds, prime, tierce, sext, nones, vespers and compline.
- **The most popular name** for a boat in 1996 was *Serenity*.
- **The name for fungal** remains found in coal is *sclerotinite*.
- **The Netherlands and** the United States both have anthems that do not mention their country's name.
- **The slash character is** called a virgule, or solidus. A URL uses slash characters, not back slash characters.
- **The stress in Hungarian** words always falls on the first syllable.

- **The term 'cop' came** from Constable on Patrol. It is from England.
- **The word accordion comes** from the German word 'akkord,' which means 'agreement, harmony.'
- **There are about 5,000 different** languages spoken on earth.
- **Trabant is the German** word for satellite.

Science

- **The search engine Google got its name** from the word 'googol', which refers to the number one with a hundred zeros after it.
- **The microwave** was invented after a researcher walked by a radar tube and a chocolate bar melted in his pocket.
- **Another name for a Microsoft Windows tutorial** is "Crash Course"!
- **Medical research has found substances in mistletoe** that can slow down tumor growth.
- **Microsoft made $16,005 in revenue** in its first year of operation.
- **Most dust particles in your house** come from dead skin.
- **There are more than 1,000 chemicals** in a cup of coffee; of these, only 26 have been tested ,and half of them caused cancer in rats.
- **A rainbow can occur only when** the sun is 40 degrees or less above the horizon.
- **Britney Spears, Anna Kournikova, Osama bin Laden,** Avril Lavigne, Michelangelo and Tonya Harding have all had computer viruses named after them.

World of Science

- **The best working light-bulb a long time ago** was a thread of sheep's wool coated with carbon.
- **A bolt of lightning can strike the earth** with a force as great as 100 million volts.

- **A cubic mile of fog is made up** of less than a gallon of water.
- **A full moon always rises** at sunset.
- **A full moon is nine times brighter** than a half moon.
- **A jumbo jet uses** 4,000 gallons of fuel to take off.
- **A metric mile is** 1,500 metres.
- **A normal raindrop falls at** about seven miles per hour.
- **A pedometer measures** walking distance.
- **A pulsar is a neutron star** and it gets its energy from its rotation.
- **The shell constitutes 12 per cent** of an egg's weight.
- **A standard grave is** 7'8 x 3'2 x 6'.
- **A wind with a speed** of 74 miles or more is designated a hurricane.
- **An iceberg contains more** heat than a match.
- **An inch of snow falling evenly** on one acre of ground is equivalent to about 2,715 gallons of water.
- **Approximately 98 per cent of software** in China is pirated.
- **At room temperature, the average air molecule** travels at the speed of a rifle bullet.
- **Bacteria, the tiniest free-living cells,** are so small that a single drop of liquid contains as many as 50 million of them.
- **Bamboo (the world's tallest grass) can** grow up to 90 cm in a day.
- **Because of the rotation of the earth, an object** can be thrown further if it is thrown west.
- **By weight, the sun is 70 per cent hydrogen,** 28 per cent helium, 1.5 per cent carbon, nitrogen and oxygen, and 0.5 per cent all other elements.
- **Diamonds are composed of just one** chemical element, carbon.
- **DuPont is the world's largest** chemical company.
- **Earth is travelling through space** at 660,000 miles per hour.

- **Experts at Intel say that microprocessor speed shall** double every 18 months for at least 10 years.
- **Gold was the first metal** to be discovered.
- **Hydrogen is the most common** atom in the universe.
- **If you attempted to count the stars in a galaxy** at a rate of one every second, it would take around 3,000 years to count them all.
- **If you yelled for eight years, seven months and six days,** you would have produced enough sound energy to heat one cup of coffee.
- **India has the world's largest stock of privately** hoarded gold.
- **India tested its first nuclear** bomb in 1974.
- **Iron nails cannot be used in oak because** the acid in the wood corrodes them.
- **It takes eight and a half minutes for** light to get from the sun to earth.
- **Japan's currency is the most** difficult to counterfeit.
- **Mercury is the only metal that is** liquid at room temperature.
- **Moisture, not air,** causes superglue to dry.
- **Rene Descartes came up with the theory** of co-ordinate geometry by looking at a fly walk across a tiled ceiling.
- **Robots in Japan pay** union dues.
- **Russia built over 10,000 miles of** railroad between 1896 and 1900.
- **Stainless steel was discovered** by accident in 1913.
- **Sunbeams that shine down through clouds** are called crepuscular rays.
- **The 'Big Bang' is said to have** created the universe.
- **The average life of a nuclear plant** is 40 years.
- **The Boeing 737 jet is** nicknamed 'Fat Albert'.
- **The Boeing 747 has been in** commercial service since 1970.

- **The colour black is produced by** the complete absorption of light rays.
- **The company Kodak is the** largest user of silver.
- **The first computer ever made** was called ENIAC.
- **The 111th element is known** as unnilenilenium.
- **The process of splitting atoms** is called fission.
- **The smallest unit of time is** the yoctosecond.
- **The speed of sound must be** exceeded to produce a sonic boom.
- **The tail section of an airplane** gives the bumpiest ride.
- **The tip of a bullwhip moves so fast that it** breaks the sound barrier; the crack of the whip is actually a tiny sonic boom.
- **The total quantity of energy in the** universe is constant.
- **The two hottest months at the equator** are March and September.
- **The Venus flytrap can eat** a whole cheeseburger.
- **Three stars make up** Orion's belt.
- **Twenty years make up** a vicennial period.
- **When glass breaks, the cracks move at** speeds up to 3,000 miles per hour.
- **You are most likely to lose your hearing** than any of the other senses if you are hit by lightning.
- **Galaxy is derived from the** ancient Greek word for milk.
- **A gap between two of the rings** of Saturn is called the Cassini Division.
- **Proxima Centauri is the nearby star** of the earth other that the sun.
- **The asteroid vesta is the only asteroid** that can be seen with the naked eye.
- **Sirius is the brightest** star in the night sky.
- **Charon is the name of Pluto's** only moon.
- **The everyday name for plants** that have the scientific classification *Graminaese* is Grasses.

- **Morphology is the study of life** shape of plants and animals.
- **Friday is named after the Scandinavian** goddess of love Frigga.
- **The month of March is named** after the Roman God of war.
- **September is not the seventh month (Septem)** but the ninth.
- **Calendar comes from Kalendae or Calendae,** the first day of each month in the ancient Roman calendar.
- **The Chinese calendar had years counted from** the accession of the emperor until 1911 AD.
- **Thursday is named after the** Norse god of thunder.
- **The 18th century French Chemist Antoine Lavoisier was** guillotined during the French Revolution.
- **W is the single letter chemical symbol** for Tungsten.
- **In computing 'pixel' is an abbreviation** for 'picture element'.
- **ENIAC was the name of the first** electronic computer.
- **The software package of Microsoft Excel** is spreadsheet.
- **Dinosaur means** Terrible Lizard.
- **Coprolites is the scientific name** for fossilized dinosaur.
- **Brontosaurus dinosaur means** 'Three horned face'.
- **Werner Heisenberg, the German scientist is famous** for his 'uncertainty principle'.
- **An epiphyte plant is one which grows** towards a light source.
- **Xerophytes are plants that live** when it is difficult to obtain water.
- **The nares is the correct scientific term** for the nostrils.
- **The oil of vitriol is** sulphuric acid.
- **Star clusters refer to** Messier numbers.

- **The island of Langerhans is** found in the ear.
- **Thomas Edison was known as** 'The Wizard of Menlo Park'.
- **Nylon was invented by** Wallace Carothers.
- **George Eastman invented** the Kodak Camera.
- **William Semple invented chewing gum in** 1869 to be a means of exercising the face.
- **An early form of calculating machine** was Napier's bones.
- **In Geometry you can find a phenomenon known** as the 'Witch of Agnesi'.
- **Brain cells are the only cells** that never re-grow.
- **The medical condition lateral epicondylitis** is commonly known as Tennis elbow.
- **The drug digitalis is obtained** from the plant foxglove.
- **T. H. Laennec in 1816 invented** the stethoscope.
- **The common name for the disease Varicella** is chicken pox.
- **The armpit is called** the axilla.
- **Ebola, a viral disease takes its name** from a river in the Republic of Congo.
- **Aspirin was the first painkiller** to be patented in 1899.
- **Red colour light has** the highest frequency.
- **A cesium atom** in an atomic clock beats 9,192,631,770 times a second.
- **A device invented as a primitive steam** engine by the Greek engineer Hero, about the time of the birth of Christ, is used today as a rotating lawn sprinkler.
- **A fully loaded supertanker travelling** at normal speed takes at least 20 minutes to stop.
- **A large flawless emerald** is worth more than a similarly large flawless diamond.

- **A lightning bolt generates temperatures** five times hotter than those found on the sun's surface.
- **A manned rocket can reach the moon** in less time than it took a stagecoach to travel the length of England.

- **A neutron star has such a powerful** gravitational pull that it can spin on its axis in one-thirtieth of a second without tearing itself apart.
- **A silicon chip a quarter-inch square** has the capacity of the original 1949 ENIAC computer, which occupied a city block.
- **A syzygy occurs** when three atronomical bodies line up.
- About seven million cars are junked each year in the US.

- **According to the Gemological Institute of America**, up until 1869 in India was the only source for diamonds in the world.
- **All organic compounds** contain carbons.
- **All snow crystals** are hexagonal.
- **All the gold produced in the past 500 years,** if melted, could be compressed into a 50-foot cube.
- **All the stars in our galaxy the Milky Way** revolve around the centre of the galaxy every 200 million years.
- **All totalled, the sunlight that strikes earth** at any given moment weighs as much as an ocean liner.
- **Almost all the helium that exists** in the world today is from natural-gas wells in the United States.

- **An enneahedron is solid** with nine faces.
- **Any free-moving liquid in outer space** will form itself into a sphere because of its surface tension.
- **Astronomers classify stars** by their spectra.

- **At any given time, there are 1,800** thunderstorms in progress over the earth's atmosphere.
- **Back in the mid to late 80s**, an IBM-compatible computer wasn't considered a hundred per cent compatible unless it could run Microsoft's Flight Simulator.
- **Carolyn Shoemaker has discovered** 32 comets and approximately 300 asteroids.
- **Clouds fly higher during** the day than the night.
- **It takes one 15-20-year-old tree** to produce 700 paper grocery bags.
- **Lab tests can detect traces of alcohol** in urine six to 12 hours after a person has stopped drinking.
- **Life on earth probably developed** in an oxygen-free atmosphere. Even today there are microorganisms that can live only in the absence of oxygen.

- **Man releases over a billion tons of pollutants** into the earth's atmosphere every year.
- **Methane gas can often be seen bubbling up** from the bottom of ponds. It is produced by the decomposition of dead plants and animals in the mud.
- **One ragweed plant can release** as many as one billion grains of pollen.
- **Orchids are grown from seeds** so small that it would take 30,000 to weigh as much as one grain of wheat.
- **South Africa produces** two-thirds of the world's gold.
- **Stars come in different colours**; hot stars give off blue light and the cooler stars give off red light.
- **The Apollo 11 had only 20 seconds** of fuel left when it landed.
- **The ashes of the metal magnesium** are heavier than magnesium itself.

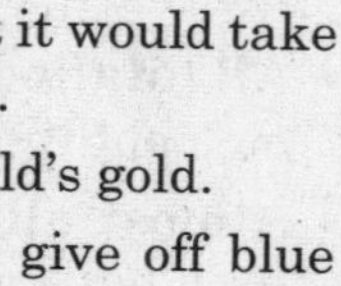

- **The bark of a redwood tree** is fireproof. Fires that occur in a redwood forest take place inside the trees.
- **The billionth digit** of PI in nine.
- **The US Bureau of Standards** says that the electron is the fastest thing in the world.

- **The CN Tower, in Toronto**, is the tallest free-standing structure in the world.
- **The colour of diamond** dust is black.
- **The condensed water vapour** left by jets in the sky is called a contrail.
- **The densest substance on earth** is the metal 'osmium.'
- **The first product Motorola** started to develop was a record player for automobiles. At that time the most well-known player on the market was the Victrola, so they called themselves Motorola.
- **The leaves of the Victorian water lily** are sometimes over six feet in diameter.
- **The metal instrument used** in shoe stores to measure feet is called the Brannock device.
- **The radio-active substance**, Americanium-241 is used in many smoke detectors.
- **The Saguaro Cactus**, found in the Southwestern United States, doesn't grow branches until it is 75 years old.
- **The strength of early lasers** was measured in Gillettes, the number of blue razor blades a given beam could puncture.
- **The US standard railroad gauge** (distance between rails) is 4 feet 8.5 inches.
- **There are five tillion trillion atoms** in one pound of iron.
- **Three astronauts manned** each Apollo flight.

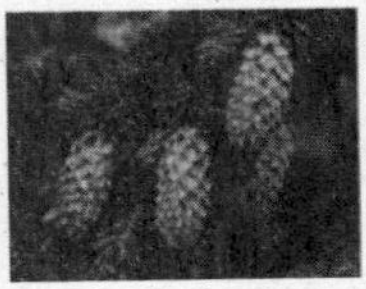

- **When CBS broadcast the first television show** in colour, no one other than CBS owned a colour television set.

- **Chess was** invented in India.
- **The world's highest cricket ground** is in Chail, Himachal Pradesh. Built in 1893 after leveling a hilltop, this cricket pitch is 2444 meters above sea level.

- **Martial Arts were** first created in India, and later spread to Asia by Buddhist missionaries.
- **The game of Snakes & Ladders** was created by the 13th century poet saint Gyandev. It was originally called 'Mokshapat'. The ladders in the game represented virtues and the snakes indicated vices. The game was played with cowrie shells and dices. In time, the game underwent several modifications, but its meaning remained the same, i.e. good deeds take people to heaven and evil to a cycle of re-births.
- **Australian Rules football** was originally designed to give cricketers something to play during the off season.
- **Canada is the only country** not to win a gold medal in the summer Olympic Games while hosting the event.
- **Dartboards are made** out of horse hairs.
- **In 1936, American track star Jesse Owens** beat a racehorse over a 100-yard course. The horse was given a head start.
- **In the United States, more Frisbee discs** are sold each year than baseballs, basketballs, and footballs combined.
- **Kite flying is a professional sport** in Thailand.
- **Nearly all Sumo wrestlers** have flat feet and big bottoms.

- **Rudyard Kipling, living in Vermont** in the 1890s, invented the game of snow golf. He would paint his golf balls red so that they could be located in the snow.
- **Sprinters on track teams** started taking a crouching start in 1908.
- **The game of squash originated** in the United Kingdom.
- **The national sport of Japan** is sumo wrestling.
- **There are at least two sports** in which the team has to move backwards to win – tug of war and rowing and swimming (back stroke).
- **Three consecutive strikes in bowling** is called a Turkey.
- **Tokyo has the world's biggest** bowling alley.
- **Tug of war was an Olympic event** between 1900 and 1920.
- **Badminton used** to be called 'poona'.
- **In the Raj some called** badminton 'phool khel'.
- **A baseball has** exactly 108 stitches.
- **Michael Jordan makes more money** from Nike annually than all of the Nike factory workers in Malaysia combined.
- **The theme song of the Harlem Globetrotters** is 'Sweet Georgia Brown'.
- **The bowling ball** was invented in 1862.
- **Americans spend more than $630 million** a year on golf balls.
- **Before 1850, golf balls were made of** leather and stuffed with feathers.
- **In the US**, there are more than 10,000 golf courses.
- **There are three golf balls** sitting on the moon.
- **There are 336 dimples** on a regular golf ball.
- **A hockey puck** is one inch thick.
- **The five Olympic rings** represent the continents.
- **Football is played in more countries** than any other sport.

- **Steffi Graf won her Grand Slam** in tennis in 1988.
- **Anise is the scent on the artificial rabbit** that is used in greyhound races.
- **A forfeited game in baseball** is recorded as a 9-0 score. In American football it is recorded as a 1-0 score.

- **Four men in the history of boxing** have been knocked out in the first 11 seconds of the first round.
- **Morihei Ueshiba, founder of Aikido**, once pinned a Sumo wrestler using only a single finger.
- **Pole vault poles used to be stiff**. Now they bend which allows the vaulter to go much higher.
- ***Sports Illustrated* has the largest sports** magazine circulation.
- **The 1900 Olympics** were held in Paris, France.
- **The only bone not broken so far** during any ski accident is one located in the inner ear.
- **There are six hoops** on an Association croquet court.
- **Olympic badminton rules** say that the birdie has to have exactly 14 feathers.
- **Fifty-six million people** go to the Major League baseball each year.
- **Baseball games between college teams** have been played since the Civil War.
- **Baseball was the first sport** to be pictured on the cover of *Sports Illustrated* magazine.
- **Baseball's home plate** is 17 inches wide.
- **Before 1859, baseball umpires** used to sit on rocking chairs behind the home plate.
- **It takes about eight seconds for a baseball bat** to be made in a baseball bat factory.
- **The first formal rules for playing the sport of baseball** required the winning team to score 21 runs.
- **Basketball was invented by Canadian James Naismith** in 1891.

- **In the movie *Toy Story*, the carpet design** in Sid's hallway is the same as the carpet design in *The Shinning.*
- **An American football** has four seams.
- **OJ Simpson had a severe case of rickets** and wore leg braces when he was a child.

- **The Super Bowl is broadcast in 182 countries**. That is more than 88 per cent of the countries in the world.
- **The only person ever to play golf on the moon** was Alan Shepard. They never found the ball.
- **The Tom Thumb golf course** was the first miniature golf courses in the United States. It was built it 1929 in Chattanooga, Tennessee by John Garnet Carter.

- **The United States Golf Association** (USGA) was founded in 1894 as the governing body of golf in the United States.
- **The Baltimore Orioles** play Baseball.
- **The fastest swimming stroke** is the *Australian crawl.*
- **Muirfield village, Ohio,** the course is called 'Course that jack built'.
- **An 'Epee' is used** in fencing.
- **Monica Seles was stabbed by** a Steffi Graf fan in April, 1993.
- **A filly is declared a** mare at the age of five.
- **A *cleek* is the Scottish term** for a golf iron.
- **180 is the higest score** you can score with three darts.
- **The game of polo is** divided into 'chukkers'.

World of Business

- **Business.com is currently** the most expensive domain name sold for $7.5 million.
- **Nylon is made from** coal and petroleum.
- **Oil tycoon, John D. Rockefeller**, was the world's first billionaire.
- **The first domain name** ever registered was Symbolics.com.
- **The first product that Sony came out** with was the rice cooker.
- **The first product that the toy company Mattel** came out with was picture frames.
- **When Scott Paper Company first** started manufacturing toilet paper they did not put their name on the product because of embarrassment.
- **IBM's motto** is 'Think'.
- **It takes about 63,000 trees to make** the newsprint for the average Sunday edition of the New York Times.
- **Nestle is the largest company** in Switzerland, yet more then 98 per cent of its revenue comes from outside the country.
- **Organised crime is estimated** to account for 10% of the United States 'national income.
- **Sixty per cent of big-firm executives** say the cover letter is as important or more important then the resume itself when you're looking for a new job.

- **The largest employer in the world** is the Indian railway system, employing over a million people.
- **The sale of vodka** makes up 10 per cent of Russian Government income.

List of Top 10 Billionaires of India By Forbes Magazine

- **Mukesh Ambani:** Total wealth of 27 Arab Dollars.
- **Lakshmi Mittal:** Total wealth of 26.1 Arab Dollars.
- **Azim Premji:** Total wealth of 17.6 Arab Dollars.
- **Shashi and Ravi:** Total wealth of 15 Arab Dollars.
- **Savitri Jindal:** Total wealth of 14.4 Arab Dollars.
- **Anil Ambani:** Total wealth of 13.3 Arab Dollars.
- **Gautam Adani:** Total wealth of 10.7 Arab Dollars.
- **Kushal Pal Singh:** Total wealth of 9.2 Arab Dollars.
- **Sunil Mittal:** Total wealth of 8.6 Arab Dollars.
- **Kumarmangalam Birla:** Total wealth of 8.5 Arab Dollars.

More Interesting Facts Related to Mukesh Ambani

- **Mukesh Ambani** to be World's Richest Man by 2014!
- **$40 Million Wealth** of Ambani Brothers!
- **Mukesh Ambani's Multi-Million Dollar** House 'Antilia'

Antilia

- **The house (called Antilla)** is being valued at Rupees 4000 crore and will be 173 metres tall.
- **3 helipads on top**. Mumbai Corporation has not given permission for making this operational yet.
- **Hanging gardens** within the structure

- **Swimming pool** within the structure
- **A two storey health centre**
- **Parking space for 168 cars** (6 floors). I initially thought that meant there will be a mini office in the building but apparently that is not the case. All these cars will belong to Mukesh Ambani! He drives an 8 crore Maybach.

The 8 million Dollar Car

- **A floor exclusively for servicing** these automobiles within the building.
- **A floor for home theatre** – sitting capacity of 50
- **Most absurd of all, the house will have a staff of 600** (sic) to do the maintenance activities.
- **That gives a ratio of 1:100 for people living** in the house and those who are paid to take care of it. The six lucky (?) ones are the man himself, his wife, his 3 children and his mother Kokilaben.
- **Mukesh bought the property** in 2002. So he has not spent anywhere close to the $1 billion people are now valuing the property at.
- **Other rich tycoons** that have indulged in their residences: Mittal & Gates.

Mittal Mansion

- **The £70-million Mansion:** Lakshmi N. Mittal, Chairman and CEO, of the LNM Group, has bought a central London house for a stunning price of £70 million ($128.25 million or about Rs 560 crore).

- **The Non-Resident Indian steel magnate's** new house has thus walked into the Guinness Book of Records as the world's most expensive house.
- **The previous record for** the most expensive house was £62.7 million ($114.89 million) for a 1997 sale in Hong Kong.

- **The 12-bedroom mansion** located at the prestigious Kensington Palace Gardens has garage space for 20 cars.
- **The Kensington Palace Gardens houses** are dubbed Billionaires' Row. Nearby are Kensington Palace and the London home of the Sultan of Brunei. It is also close to Kensington Palace where Princess Diana lived.
- **Mittal, whose personal wealth** is put at £3.5 billion, is the richest Asian in the United Kingdom.

- **He also owns a £9-million mansion** on London's Bishop Avenue, and a house on Delhi's Prithviraj Road which is said to have cost him Rs 40 crore.
- **LNM also has a penthouse at Hyde Park** and houses in Surabaya, Indonesia, and in Trinidad.

Bill Gates

- **Bill Gates earns $250 every second**, that's about $20 million a day and $7.8 billion a year!
- **If he drops a thousand dollars**, he won't even bother to pick it up because in the 4 seconds it takes to pick it up, he would have already earned it back.
- **U.S.'s national debt** is about $5.62 trillion. If Bill Gates wants to pay the debt by himself; he will finish it in less than 10 years.
- **He can donate $15 to everyone** on earth and still be left with $5million for his pocket money.

- **Michael Jordan is the highest paid athlete** in the U.S. If he doesn't drink and eat, and keep his annual income at $30 million, he'll have to wait for 277 years to become as rich as Bill Gates is today.
- **If Bill Gates were a country**, he will be the 37th richest country on the earth.

- **If you change all of Bill Gate's money** to $1 bills, you can make a road from earth to moon 14 times back and forth. But you will have to make that road non-stop for 1400 years, and use a total of 713 Boeing 747 planes to transport all the money.
- **If we assume that he still can live** for another 35 years, he has to spend $6.78 million per day to finish his money before his death.

Bill Gates House

- **One of the most interesting things** you'd experience if you lived in this house is that you wear a pin containing a microchip which acts as your ID. When you walk into a room, lighting, sound, and temp controls are customized for you. Any high resolution display that you walk by will know that you're there, and your favorite art is displayed. And if you're getting a phone call, only the phone nearest to you will ring. This is all thanks to the pin with the microchip.
- **A single share of Coca-Cola stock**, purchased in 1919, when the company went public, would have been worth $92,500 in 1997.
- **NERF, the popular foam children's toy company**, doesn't actually stand for anything.

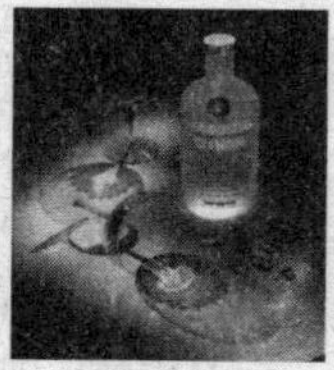

- **The sale of makes up 10 per cent** of Russian Government income.
- **Workers at Matsushita Electric Company** in Japan beat dummies of their foremen with bamboo sticks to let off steam. The Company has enjoyed 30 per cent growth for 25 consecutive years.

Places

- **160 cars can drive side by side** on the Monumental Axis in Brazil, the world's widest road.
- **At April 2000, Hong Kong** had 392,000 fax lines – one of the highest rates of business fax use in the world.
- **Buckingham Palace** has over 600 rooms.
- **Construction on the Leaning Tower** of Pisa began on 9 August, 1173.
- **Disneyland opened** in 1955.
- **Due to precipitation,** for a few weeks K2 is taller than Mt. Everest.
- **If a statue in the park** of a person on a horse has both front legs in the air, the person died in battle; if the horse has one front leg in the air, the person died as a result of wounds received in battle; if the horse has all four legs on the ground, the person died of natural causes.
- **If you come from Manchester,** you are a Mancunian.
- **If you divide the Great Pyramid's** perimeter by two times its height, you get PI to the fifteenth digit.
- **In Paris, the McDonalds big 'M'** is the only one in the world that is white, rather than yellow; it was thought that yellow was too tacky.
- **It is forbidden for Aircraft** to fly over the Taj Mahal.
- **New York's Central Park** is nearly twice the size of the entire country of Monaco.

- **Printed on the book** being held by the Statue of Liberty is 'July IV, MDCCLXXVI'.
- **Some hotels in Las Vegas** have gambling tables floating in their swimming pools.
- **The Angel Falls in Venezuela** are nearly 20 times taller than Niagra Falls.
- **The blueprints for the Eiffel Tower** covered more than 14,000 square feet of drafting paper.
- **The Great Wall** stretches for 4,160 miles across North China.
- **The height of the Eiffel Tower** varies as much as six inches depending on the temperature.
- **The name of the woman** on the statue of Liberty is Mother of Exiles.
- **The nickname** of Alcatraz Prison is 'The Rock'.
- **The oldest University** in the US is Harvard.
- **The proposed William Jefferson Clinton Presidential Library** will have a section where you must be 18 or older to read certain documents.
- **The Statue of Liberty's** mouth is three feet wide.
- **There are 102 floors** in the Empire State Building.
- **There are 296 steps** to the top of the Leaning Tower of Pisa.
- **There are 47 czars** buried within the Kremlin.
- **There are no clocks** in Las Vegas gambling casinos.
- **There is a place** in Norway called Hell.
- **There is a town** in Texas called Ding Dong.
- **There were 57 countries** involved in World War II.

Places: India

- **India is the world's** largest, oldest, continuous civilisation.
- **India never invaded any country** in her last 10000 years of history.

The Great Indian Snake Charmer

- **The World's first university** was established in Takshashila in 700 BC.
- **Sanskrit is the mother** of all the European languages. Sanskrit is the most suitable language for computer software - a report in Forbes magazine, July 1987.
- **Ayurveda is the earliest school** of medicine known to humans. Charaka, the father of medicine consolidated Ayurveda 2500 years ago.
- **The art of Navigation** was born in the river Sindhu 6000 years ago. The very word Navigation is derived from the Sanskrit word NAVGATIH. The word navy is also derived from Sanskrit 'Nou'.
- **Algebra, trigonometry** and calculus came from India.
- **Sushruta is the father** of surgery(2600 years ago).
- **When many cultures** were only nomadic forest dwellers over 5000 years ago, Indians established Harappan culture in Sindhu Valley (Indus Valley Civilization).
- **The four religions born** in India, Hinduism, Buddhism, Jainism, and Sikhism, are followed by 25% of the world's population.
- **The place value system,** the decimal system was developed in India in 100 BC.
- **India has the second largest pool** of scientists and engineers in the World.
- **India is the largest English speaking** nation in the world.

- **Martial Arts was first** developed in India.
- **India has the largest number** of post offices in the world.
- **The value of "pi"** used in mathematics was first calculated by the Indian mathematician Budhayana in 6th century.
- **Computer Software products:** India is one of the largest exporter of computer software products. It exports softwares to over 90 countries.

- **The world's largest pilgrimage destination:** India has the world's largest pilgrimage destination called the Vishnu Temple in the city of Tirupati. About an average of 30,000 people visit this temple donating about $6 million everyday.
- **Yoga: The origination of Yoga** was done 5,000 years ago in India.
- **Mosques: India** has the most number of mosques. It has 300,000 mosques which is much more than the Muslim world.
- **Christians and Jews** have been living in India since 52 A.D. and 200 B.C. respectively.

Famous Quotes on India (by non-Indians)

- **Albert Einstein said:** We owe a lot to the Indians, who taught us how to count, without which no worthwhile scientific discovery could have been made.
- **Mark Twain said:** India is, the cradle of the human race, the birthplace of human speech, the mother of history, the grandmother of legend, and the great grandmother of tradition. Our most valuable and most instructive materials in the history of man are treasured up in India only.
- **French scholar Romain Rolland said:** If there is one place on the face of earth where all the dreams of living men have found a home from the very earliest days when man began the dream of existence, it is India.

- **There are 3.22 millions of Indians** in USA (1.5% of population).

More Interesting Facts about India

- **The name 'India'** is derived from the River Indus, the valleys around which were the home of the early settlers. The Aryan worshippers referred to the river Indus as the Sindhu.
- **The Persian invaders converted it into Hindu.** The name 'Hindustan' combines Sindhu and Hindu and thus refers to the land of the Hindus.

- **The World's First Granite Temple** is the Brihadeswara Temple at Tanjavur, Tamil Nadu. The shikhara of the temple is made from a single 80-tonne piece of granite. This magnificent temple was built in just five years, (between 1004 AD and 1009 AD) during the reign of Rajaraja Chola.

- **The game of Snakes & Ladders** was created by the 13th century poet saint Gyandev. It was originally called 'Mokshapat'. The ladders in the game represented virtues and the snakes indicated vices. The game was played with cowrie shells and dices. In time, the game underwent several modifications, but its meaning remained the same, i.e. good deeds take people to heaven and evil to a cycle of re-births.
- **Bhaskaracharya rightly calculated** the time taken by the earth to orbit the Sun hundreds of years before the astronomer Smart. According to his calculation, the time taken by the Earth to orbit the Sun was 365.258756484 days.
- **Algebra, Trigonometry and Calculus** also originated in India. Quadratic Equations were used by Sridharacharya in the 11th century. The largest numbers the Greeks and the Romans used were 106 whereas Hindus used numbers as big as 10*53 (i.e. 10 to the power of 53) with specific names as early as 5000 B.C.during the Vedic period.Even today, the largest used number is Terra: 10*12(10 to the power of 12).

- **Until 1896, India** was the only source of diamonds in the world.
- **The Baily Bridge** is the highest bridge in the world. It is located in the Ladakh valley between the Dras and Suru rivers in the Himalayan mountains. It was built by the Indian Army in August 1982.
- **Usage of anaesthesia** was well known in ancient Indian medicine. Detailed knowledge of anatomy, embryology, digestion, metabolism,physiology, etiology, genetics and immunity is also found in many ancient Indian texts.

- **India exports software** to 90 countries.
- **Islam is India's** and the world's second largest religion.
- **The oldest European church** and synagogue in India are in the city of Cochin. They were built in 1503 and 1568 respectively.
- **The largest religious building** in the world is Angkor Wat, a Hindu Temple in Cambodia built at the end of the 11th century.
- **Sikhism originated in the Holy city** of Amritsar in Punjab. Famous for housing the Golden Temple, the city was founded in 1577.
- **Varanasi, also known as Benaras,** was called "the Ancient City" when Lord Buddha visited it in 500 B.C., and is the oldest, continuously inhabited city in the world today.
- **India provides safety for more than 300,000** refugees originally from Sri Lanka, Tibet, Bhutan, Afghanistan and Bangladesh, who escaped to flee religious and political persecution.
- **India is about 1/3 the size of the United States,** yet it is the second most populous country in the world, with a population of 1,166,079,217. India is the seventh largest country in the world, at 1.27 million square miles.
- **The Kumbh Mela (or Grand Pitcher Festival)** is a huge Hindu religious festival that takes place in India every 12 years. In 2001, 60 million people attended, breaking the record for the world's biggest gathering. The mass of people was photographed from space by a satellite.
- **To avoid polluting the elements** (fire, earth, water, air), followers of Zoroastrianism in India don't bury their dead, but instead leave bodies in buildings called "Towers of Silence" for the vultures to pick clean. After the bones dry, they are swept into a central well.

- **Cows can be found freely** wandering the streets of India's cities. They are considered sacred and will often wear a *tilak,* a Hindu symbol of good fortune. Cows are considered one of humankind's seven mothers because she offers milk as does one's natural mother.
- **Dancing is one of India's** most highly developed arts and was an integral part of worship in the inner shrines of every temple. It is notable for its expressive hand movements.
- Rabies is endemic in India. Additionally, "Delhi Belly" or diarrhea is commonplace due to contaminated drinking water.
- **Many Indian wives will** never say her husband's name aloud, as it is a sign of disrespect. When addressing him, the wife will use several indirect references, such as "ji" or "look here" or "hello," or even refer to him as the father of her child.
- **A widow is considered bad luck**—otherwise, her husband wouldn't have died. Elderly women in the village might call a widow "the one who ate her husband." In some orthodox families, widows are not allowed near newlyweds or welcomed at social gatherings.
- **India is the birthplace of chess.** The original word for "chess" is the Sanskrit *chaturanga,* meaning "four members of an army"—which were mostly likely elephants, horses, chariots, and foot soldiers.

- **The Indian flag has three horizontal bands of colour:** saffron for courage and sacrifice, white for truth and peace, and green for faith, fertility, and chivalry. An emblem of a wheel spinning used to be in the center of the white band, but when India gained independence, a Buddhist *dharma chakra,* or wheel of life, replaced the spinning wheel.
- **The temples of Khajuraho** are famous for their erotic sculptures and are one of the most popular tourist attractions in India. Scholars still debate the purpose of such explicit

portrayals of sexual intercourse, which sometimes involves animals.

- **The earliest cotton** in the world was spun and woven in India. Roman emperors would wear delicate cotton from India that they would call "woven winds." Mogul emperors called the fabrics "morning dew" and "cloth of running water."
- **The Himalayas**—from the Sanskrit *hima*, meaning "snow," and *alaya*, meaning "abode"—are found in the north of India. They extend 1,500 miles and are slowly growing taller, by almost an inch (2.5 cm) a year. Several ancient Indian monasteries are found nestled in the grandeur of these mountains.
- **India is the world's** largest producer of dried beans, such as kidney beans and chickpeas. It also leads the world in banana exports; Brazil is second.
- **In India, grasping** one's ears signifies repentance or sincerity.
- **Indians hold prominent places** both internationally and in the United States. For example, the co-founder of Sun Microsystems (Vinod Khosla), the creator of the Pentium chip (Vinod Dahm), the founder/creator of Hotmail (Sabeer Bhatia), and the GM of Hewlett-Packard (Rajiv Gupta) are all Indian.
- **Alexander the Great of Macedon (356-323 B.C.)** was one of the first important figures to bring India into contact with the West. After his death, a link between Europe and the East would not be restored until Portuguese explorer Vasco da Gama (1460-1524) landed in Calicut, India, in 1498.
- **The British Raj, or British rule,** lasted from 1858 to 1947 (although they had a strong presence in India since the 1700s). British influence is still seen in Indian architecture, education system, transportation, and politics. Many of India's worst famines are associated with British rule in India.
- **About 80% of Indians are Hindu.** Muslims are the largest minority in India and form approximately 13% of the country's population. In fact, India has the third largest population of Muslims in the world, after Indonesia and Pakistan.

- **India has the world's largest movie industry,** based in the city of Mumbai (known as the "City of Dreams"). The B in "Bollywood" comes from Bombay, the former name for Mumbai. Almost all Bollywood movies are musicals.
- **Mumbai (Bombay) is India's largest city,** with a population of 15 million. In 1661, British engineers built a causeway uniting all seven original islands of Bombay into a single landmass.
- **Mohandas K. Gandhi (1869-1948)** is known around the world as Mahatma, which is an honorific title meaning "Great Soul" in the ancient Indian language of Sanskrit. He devoted his life to free India from British rule peacefully and based his campaign on civil disobedience. His birthday, October 2, is a national holiday. He was assassinated in 1948.
- **The lotus is sacred** to both Hindus and Buddhists. The Bahá'í house of worship in Delhi, known as the "Lotus Temple," is shaped like a lotus flower with 27 gigantic "petals" that are covered in marble.

The Lotus temple is one of the most visited temples in the world, with over 50 million visitors per year

- **The banyan, or Indian fig tree,** is considered a symbol of immortality and is mentioned in many Indian myths and legends. This self-renewing plant is India's national tree.
- **Marigold flowers are used** as decoration for Hindu **marriages** and are a symbol of good fortune and happiness.
- **The official name of India** is the Republic of India. The name "India" derives from the River Indus, which most likely is derived from the Sanskrit *sindhu,* meaning "river." The official Sanskrit name of India is *Bharat,* after the legendary king in the epic *Mahabharata.*
- **Introduced by the British, cricket is India's** most popular sport. Hockey is considered the national sport, and the Indian field hockey team proudly won Olympic gold in 1928.

- **The national fruit of India is the mango.** The national bird is the peacock, which was initially bred for food.

- **Most historians agree that** the first recorded account of plastic surgery is found in ancient Indian Sanskrit texts.
- **Hindi and English** are the official languages of India. The government also recognizes 17 other languages (Assamese, Bengali, Gujarati, Nepali, Manipuri, Konkani, Kannada, Kashmiri, Malayalam, Marathi, Oriya, Punjabi, Sanskrit, Sindhi, Tamil, Telugu, and Urdu). Apart from these languages, about 1,652 dialects are spoken in the country.
- **India's pastoral communities** are largely dependent on dairy and have made India the largest milk-producing country in the world.
- **India has the world's** third largest road network at 1.9 million miles. It also has the world's second largest rail network, which is the world's largest civilian employer with 16 million workers.
- **Rivers have played a vital role in India's** popular culture and folklore—they have been worshipped as goddesses because they bring water to an otherwise dry land. Bathing in the Ganges in particular is thought to take away a person's sins. It is not unusual to spread a loved one's ashes in the Ganges.

Though the Ganges is one of the dirtiest rivers in the world, bathing in the river is thought to wash away one's sins

- **Raziya Sultana (1205-1240)** was the first woman leader of India. She was considered a great leader, though she ruled for only three years before being murdered.
- **Most Indians rinse their hands, legs,** and face before eating a meal. It is considered polite to eat with the right hand, and women eat after everyone is finished. Wasting food is considered a sin.
- **During the Vedic era in India,** horse sacrifice sanctioned the sovereignty of the king.
- **It is traditional to wear white,** not black, to a funeral in India. Widows will often wear white in contrast to the colorful clothes of married or single women.

- **All of India** is under a single time zone.
- **On India's Independence Day, August 15, 1947,** the country was split into India and Pakistan. The partition displaced 1.27 million people and resulted in the death of several hundred thousand to a million people.
- **India experiences six seasons:** summer, autumn, winter, spring, summer monsoon, and winter monsoon.
- **India is the world's** largest tea producer, and tea (chai) is its most popular beverage.
- **The Taj Mahal ("crown palace")** was built by Mughal Emperor Shah Jahan (1592-1666) for his beloved wife Mumtaz Mahal (1593-1631). This architectural beauty has been called "marbled embroidery" for its intricate workmanship. It took 22,000 workmen 22 years to complete it.

According to legend, to prevent the builders from ever replicating the beauty of the Taj Mahal, their hands were cut off

- **Alexander the Great invaded India partly** because he wanted to solve the mystery of the "ocean," which he had been told was a huge, continuous sea that flowed in a circle around the land. When he reached the Indian Ocean, he sacrificed some bulls to Poseidon for leading him to his goal.
- **Greek sculpture strongly influenced** many portrayals of Indian gods and goddess, particularly after the conquest of Alexander the Great around 330B.C. In fact, early Indian gods had Greek features and only later did distinct Indian styles emerge.
- **Chandragupta Maurya (340-290 B.C.),** a leader in India who established the Mauryan Empire (321-185 B.C.), was guarded by a band of women on horseback.
- **When the first independent prime minister of India, pacifist Jawaharlal Nehru (1889-1964),** was featured in Vogue, his distinctive close fitting, single-breasted jacket briefly

became an important fashion statement for the Mod movement in the West. Named the Nehru jacket, the prime minister's coat was popularized by the Beatles and worn by such famous people as Johnny Carson (1925-2005) and Sammy Davis Jr. (1925-1990).

- **India has won five Miss World titles** and two Miss Universe titles.

- **Since 1990, Miss Venezuela and Miss India** are rivals in the beauty world.
- **1966: London, England. Miss India,** Rita Faria, was elected Miss World.
- **1994: Manila (Philippines).** Miss India, Shusmita Sen, was crowned Miss Universe.

- **1994: Sun City (South Africa).** Miss India, Aishwarya Rai, won the Miss World pageant.
- **1997: Mahe, Seychelles.** Miss India, Diana Hayden, was elected Miss Asia and Miss World.
- **1999: London, England.** India´s Yukta Mookhey won the Miss World title.
- **2000: Nicosia, Cypruss.** Miss India, Lara Dutta, was crowned Miss Universe.
- **2000: London, England.** India´s Priyanka Chopra was crowned Miss Asia and Miss World.

New Delhi: Fun Facts

- **Delhi is the capital of India,** its third largest city, and the industrial hub of northern India. In addition to being the epicenter of power, Delhi is the second most widely used entry point into the country....

Green Facts:

- **Delhi is one of the 'greenest'** cities in the world with a green cover of almost 20%.

- **The entire public transport** of the city runs on environment friendly Compressed Natural Gas.

Interesting Facts:

- **Qutub Minar in Delhi** is the world's tallest brick minaret.
- **The walled city of Delhi** originally had fourteen gates. Five are still standing. Here's the provenance behind their names. Ajmeri Gate: Facing Ajmer in Rajasthan; Lahori Gate: Facing Lahore in Pakistan. Kashmiri Gate: Pointing North to Kashmir. Delhi Gate: Road to earlier cities of Delhi Turkman Gate: Named after pious saint Hazrat Shah Turkam.

- **In between the rubble of the fifth city of Delhi** – Feroz Shah Kotla stands the 3 century B.C. Ashokan Pillar. Emperor Feroz Shah Tughlaq brought this 27 tonne pillar to Delhi from Topar in Ambala, where the great Emperor Ashoka erected it.

Weird Fact:

- **Delhi has an** International Toilet museum.

Spicy Fact:

- **Khari Baoli is the Asia's** largest wholesale spice market. A must visit for the once-in-a-lifetime overdose of spice.

Random Facts:

- **Traffic in Delhi is like traffic in London.** Drivers sit on the right side of the car.
- **Three-wheeled contraptions called Autos** are a great way to see the city over short distances.
- Delhi has a rail museum with steam-age behemoths.

Odds and Ends

The Odds Against Various Eventualities

- **Being struck by lightning:** 1 in 10 million.
- **Being killed by a bee sting:** 1 in 6 million.
- **Becoming an alcoholic** if you drink regularly: 1 in 10.

Maniacs

- **Kleptomaniac** (person obsessed with stealing).
- **Chionomaniac** (snow).
- **Ablutomaniac** (bathing).
- **Timbromaniac** (stamps).
- **Cynomaniac** (dogs).
- **Ailuromaniac** (cats).
- **Ichthyomaniac** (fish).
- **Oniomaniac** (buying).
- **Arithomaniac** (counting).
- **Philopatridomaniac** (homesickness).
- **Bruxomaniac** (grinding teeth).
- **Klazomaiac** (shouting).
- **Catapedamaniac** (jumping from high places).
- **Onychotillomaniac** (picking nails).
- **Cresomaniac** (personal wealth).
- **Phagomaniac** (food).
- **Titillomaniac** (scratching).

- **Erythromaniac** (blushing).
- **Dromomaniac** (traveling).

Murphy's Law

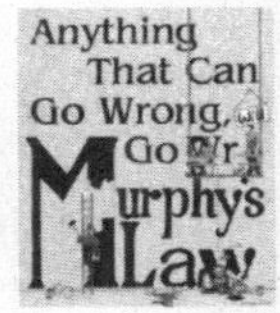

- **Anything that can go** wrong will go wrong.
- **The first place to look** for something is the last place you would expect to find it.
- **When someone says,** "It's not the money, It's the principal," nine times out of ten, it's money.
- **Whenever you make** a journey by bicycle, it's always more uphill than downhill.
- **As soon as you mention** (something, a) if it' good, it goes away; b) if it's bad, it happens.
- **You never find something** until you replace it.
- **When the train you** are on is late, the bus to take you home from the station will be on time.
- **If an experience works,** something has gone wrong.
- **If always rains when** you've just washed your car, but washing your car to make it rain won't work.
- **When you dial a wrong number,** it's never busy.
- **Checks get lost in the mail,** but bills never do.
- **In a supermarket the other** lines always move faster than yours.
- **Illness always start on** a Friday evening....but end on a Monday morning.
- **Friends come and go,** but enemies accumulate.
- **The severity of an itch** is inversely proportional to how easy it is to scratch.
- **The only way to get** a bank loan is to prove you don't need one.

Odds And Ends

- **George Washington** is the only man whose birthday is a legal holiday in every state of the US as a few years ago.

- **Impotence is legal grounds** for divorce in 24 American states.
- **In England during Queen** Victoria's reign, it was illegal to be a homosexual but not a lesbian. The reason being that when the Queen was approving the law she wouldn't believe that women would do that.
- **In Hartford, Connecticut,** it is illegal for a husband to kiss his wife on Sundays.
- **In Sweden, while prostitution** is legal, it is illegal for anyone to use the services of a prostitute.
- **In California, it is illegal** to eat oranges while bathing.
- **It is illegal to grow** or sell pork in Israel.
- **Abraham Lincoln's ghost** is said to haunt the White House.
- **Adolf Hitler had planned** to change the name of Berlin to Germania.
- **Adolf Hitler was Time's** man of the year for 1938.
- **Albert Einstein was offered** the presidency of Israel in 1952.
- **Alexander Graham Bell made** a talking doll that said 'mama' when he was a young boy in Scotland.
- **Alexander Graham Bell never** telephoned his wife or mother. They were both deaf.
- **Alexander the Great** was an epileptic.
- **Alexander the Great** was tutored by Aristotle.
- **Alfred Hitchcock** did not have a belly button.
- **American media mogul** Ted Turner owns 5 per cent of New Mexico.
- **Benito Mussolini** would ward off the evil eye by touching his testicles.
- **Charles Dickens never finished** his schooling.
- **Charles Chaplin once won** third prize in a Charlie Chaplin lookalike contest.

- **Clark Gable used to** shower more than four times a day.
- **Every time Beethoven sat** down to write music, he poured ice water over his head.
- **Galileo became totally blind** just before his death. This is probably because of his constant gazing at the sun through his telescope.
- **Gandhi took dance** and music lessons in his late teens.
- **Henry Ford flatly stated** that "history is bunk."
- **Hitler and Napoleon both** had only one testicle.
- **Hitler was claustrophobic.** The elevator leading to his Eagles' nest in the Austrian Alps was mirrored so it would appear larger and more open.
- **Isaac Newton dropped out** of school when he was a teenager.
- **Leonardo da Vinci** spent 12 years painting Mona Lisa's lips.
- **Mae West was once** dubbed 'The statue of Libido'.
- **Marie Curie, the Nobel Prize-winning** scientist who discovered radium, died on 4th July, 1934 of radiation poisoning.
- **Mark Twain was born** in 1835 when Halley's comet returned.
- **Mozart is buried in** an unmarked pauper's grave.
- **Mozart wrote the nursery** rhyme 'Twinkle Twinkle, Little Star' at the age of five.
- **Napoleon conducted his battle plans** in a sandbox.
- **Napoleon favoured mathematicians** and physical scientists but excluded humanists from his circle, believing them to be troublemakers.

- **Napoleon Bonaparte** was afraid of cats.
- **Nobody knows where the** body of Voltaire is. It was stolen in the nineteenth century and has

never been recovered. The theft was discovered in 1864, when the tomb was opened and found empty.

- **Pluto, the astrological sign for death,** was directly above Dallas, Texas when JFK was born.
- **Sherlock Holmes** had a smarter brother named Mycroft.
- **Sir Isaac Newton was** an ordained priest in the Church of England.
- **Sir Isaac Newton was** only 23 years old when he discovered the law of universal gravitation.
- **Socrates committed suicide** by drinking the poison hemlock.
- **Socrates left** no writings of his own.
- **The world record for** most children to one mother is 69 children.
- **There are about 15,000 people** in the US over the age of 100.
- **Vincent Van Gogh committed** suicide while painting Wheat Field with Crows.
- **According to a British law passed in 1845,** attempting to commit suicide was a capital offence. Offenders could be hanged for trying.
- **Christmas was** once illegal in England.
- **Duelling is legal** in Paraguay as long as both parties are registered blood donors.
- **In Athens, Greece,** a driver's licence can be taken away by law if the driver is deemed either 'unbathed' or 'poorly dressed'.
- **In Cleveland, Ohio** it is illegal to catch mice without a hunting licence.
- **In Helsinki, Finland, instead** of giving parking tickets, the police usually deflate tyres.
- **In Italy, it is illegal** to make coffins out of anything except nutshells or wood.
- **In Texas, it is illegal** to put graffiti on someone else's cow.

- **In the UK, there** is no Act of Parliament making it illegal to commit murder. Murder is only illegal due to legal precedent.
- **It is against the law** to stare at the mayor of Paris.
- **In Sweden,** it is illegal to train a seal to balance a ball on its nose.
- **In Arizone,** it is illegal to hunt camels.
- **It is illegal,** in Malaysia, for restaurants to substitute toilet paper as table napkins. Repeat offenders go to jail.

- **It used to be law** in France that children's names had to be taken from an official government list.
- **In Iceland,** it was once against the law to have a pet dog in a city.
- **In one city in Switzerland,** it was once against the law to slam your car door.
- **Pennsylvania was the first colony** to legalise witchcraft.
- **According to the United States Refuse Act of 1889,** every industrial discharge into bodies of water since 1899 has been a crime.
- **Every citizen of Kentucky** is required by law to take a bath at least once a year.
- **If you live in Michigan,** it is illegal to put a skunk in your boss's desk.
- **In Indiana,** it is illegal to ride public transportation for at least 30 minutes after eating garlic.
- **In Minnesota,** it is illegal for woman to be dressed up as Santa Claus on city streets.
- **In some part of Alabama,** United States, it is illegal to carry a comb in your pocket.
- **In the 1985 Boise, Idaho,** mayoral election, there was four write-in votes for Mr. Potatohead.
- **In Oklahoma,** it is against the law to hunt whale.
- **It is illegal for** boys in 9th grade to grow a moustache in Binghamton, New York.

- **In a church in Omaha,** Nebraska, it's against the law to burp or sneeze.
- **In Kansas, it's against** the law to catch fish with your bare hands.
- **Most burglaries** occur in the winter.
- **Under the law of** Mississippi, there's no such thing as a female Peeping Tom.
- **There is a person** in New Orleans with the name Luscious Pea.
- **Al Capone's brother** was a town sheriff.
- **Albert Einstein last** words were in German. Since the attending nurse did not understand German, his last words will never be known.
- **Aristotle thought that** blood cooled the brain.

- **Astronaut Neil Armstrong** stepped on the moon with his left foot first.
- **Benjamin Franklin** was the first head of the United States Post Office.
- **Benjamin Franklin wanted the turkey,** not the eagle, to be the US national symbol.
- **Buzz Aldrin** was the first man to pee his pants on the moon.

- **Charles de Gaulle's** final words were 'It hurts'.
- **Catherine de Medici** was the first woman in Europe to use tobacco. She took it in a mixture of snuff.
- **Christopher Columbus** had blond hair.
- **Dr. Jekyll's** first name is Henry.
- **Despite his great scientific** and artistic achievement, Leonardo da Vinci was most proud of his ability to bend iron with his bare hands.
- **Gandhi** was born in 1869.
- **Genghis Khan** started out as a goatherd.

- **Hans Christin Anderson,** creator of fairy tales, was word-blind. He never learned to spell correctly, and his publishers always had errors.
- **Howdy Doody** had 48 freckles.
- **John D Rockefeller** was the first billionaire in the US.
- **John Hancock** was the only one of 50 signatories of the Declaration of Independence who actually signed it in July.
- **John Lennon's** middle name was Winston.
- **John Lennon's** first girlfriend was named Thelma Pickles.
- **Julie Nixon,** daughter of Richard Nixon, married David Eisenhower, grandson of Dwight Eisenhower.
- **Lee Harvey Oswald's** body tag was auctioned off for $6,800.
- **Leon Trotsky,** the seminal Russian Communist, was assassinated in Mexico with an icepick.
- **Li Hung-chang** is the father of Chop Suey.
- **Mel Blanc** (the voice of Bugs Bunny) was allergic to carrots.
- **Michelangelo carved** the famed Medici tombs in Florence.
- **More than 100 descendants** of Johann Sebastian Bach have been cathedral organists.
- **Oliver Cromwell was hanged** and decapitated two years after his death.

- **Orville Wright was involved** in the first aircraft accident. His passenger, a Frenchman, was killed.
- **Salvador Dali once arrived** at an art exhibition in a limousine filled with turnips.
- **Samuel Clemens,** aka Mark Twain, smoked 40 cigars a day for the last years of his life.
- **Shakespeare spelled his own** name in several different ways.
- **Sherlock Holmes's arch** enemy was Professor Moriarty.

- **Socrates committed** suicide by drinking the poison hemlock.
- **St Stephan** is the patron saint of bricklayers.
- **Stalin's left foot** had webbed toes, and his left arm was noticeably shorter.
- **The first man to return** safely from space was Yuri Gagarin.
- **The Mongol Emperor Genghis Khan's** original name was Temuji.
- **There is a prison in Ossining,** New York named 'Sing Sing'.
- **Thomas Edison** had a collection of over 5,000 birds.

- **Vincent Van Gogh** decided to become an artist when he was 27 years old.
- **Valentina Tereshkova** was the first woman to enter space.
- **Walt Disney's autograph** bears no resemblance to the famous Disney logo.
- **Walt Disney** died out of lung cancer.
- **When Einstein was inducted** as an American, he attended the ceremony without socks.
- **Warren Beatty and Shirley MacLaine** are brother and sister.
- **When young and impoverished,** Pablo Picasso kept warm by burning his own paintings.
- **Chinese red** is red.
- **There are three Graces** in Greek mythology.
- **Luke is the patron** saint of doctors.
- ***Sextiles, Oostmaand, Weodmonathy,*** and *Themider* are old names of the month of August.
- **Woodrow Wilson was the** 20th century US President who married while in office.
- **The first motorbike** was made of wood.

- **Dutch painter Vincent Van Gogh** cut off his left ear. His Self-portrait was the bandaged because he painted the mirror image.
- **Entomophobia** is the fear of insects.
- **Eosophobia** is the fear of dawn.
- **Ernest Vincent Wright** wrote the 50,000 – word novel Gatsby without any word containing 'e'.

- ***Essay* in French** means 'to try, attempt'.
- **Every minute 47** bibles are sold or distributed throughout the world.
- **Forget-me-not:** According to German legend this flower gets its name from the last words of a knight, who was drowned while trying to pick some from the riverside for his lady.
- **Ghosts appear** in four Shakespearian plays; Julius Caesar, Richard III, Hamlet and Macbeth.
- **Great Britain** was the first country to issue postage stamps. Hence, the postage stamps of Britain are the only stamps in the world not to bear the name of the country of origin. However, every stamp carries a relief image or a silhouette of the monarch's head instead.
- **Groaking is to watch** people eating in the hope that they will offer you some.
- **Papaphobia** is the fear of popes.

- **People didn't always say** hello when they answered the phone. When the first regular phone service was established in 1878, people said *Ahoy*.

- **Phobatrivaphobia is fear of** trivia about phobias.
- **Quisling is the only** word in the English language to start with 'quis'.
- **Sekkusu** is sex in Japanese.
- **The third year of marriage** is called the leather anniversary.
- **The idiom "everything but the kitchen sink"** originates around the time of World War II.
- **An "armchair critic" or "armchair quarterback"** may be quick to dole out advice, but is unlikely to show any action to back it up.
- **You can also advise someone to** "keep your hands out of my cookie jar" if you don't want them interfering in your business.
- **The hand that "rules the world rocks the cradle":** This phrase originates in a poem by William Ross Wallace.
- **"Over the counter" usually refers to** medication that can be sold without a prescription.
- **"Cash on the barrelhead" refers to** paying for goods or services immediately, without using credit or a tab.
- **Paying someone "under the table"** may refer to business or dinner meetings in which a bribe or a secret payment is passed under the table.
- **"Cut a rug" is a slang** expression for dancing.
- **"Taking a bath" on a deal** means you are losing a large sum of money, so in addition to getting cleaned up, "taking a bath" could leave you cleaned out.

Household Trivia

- **A coat hanger** is 44 inches long if straightened.
- **A 60-minute** cassette contains 565 feet of tape.
- **A good typist** can strike 20 keys in a second.
- **Camera shutter** speed 'B' stands for bulb.
- **Ketchup is excellent** for cleaning brass, especially tarnished or corroded brass.
- **Kleenex tissues were originally** used as filters in gas masks.
- **Mosquito repellants do not repel.** They hide you. The spray blocks the mosquito's sensors so they do not know you are there.
- **Oral-B is a combination** of oral hygiene and the letter B, which stands for the world 'better'.
- **Rubber bands last longer** when refrigerated.
- **Some Eskimos have been** known to use refrigerators to keep their food from freezing.
- **The ace of spades** in a playing card deck symbolizes death.
- **The average person looks** at eight houses before buying one.
- **The average lead pencil** will draw a line 35 miles long or write approximately 50,000 English worlds.
- **The average mouse pad** is 8.75 inches by 7.5 inches.

- **The end of a hammer,** opposite the striking end, is called a peen.
- **The most popular contact** lens colour is blue.
- **The plastic things** on the end of shoelaces are called *aglets*.
- **The playing card** 'nine of hearts' is considered the symbol of love.
- **The ridges on the** sides of coins are called reeding or milling.
- **The side of a** hammer is a cheek.
- **Neck ties were first** worn in Croatia. that's why they were called cravats (cro-vats).
- **On average, most people** button their shirts upwards.

- **The armhole in clothing** is called an *armsaye*.
- **Three teaspoons make up** one tablespoon.
- **The hula hoop was** the biggest selling toy in 1957.